THE CMO MANIFESTO

A 100-Day Action Plan for Marketing Change Agents

To Andrew —

Continued success to you in
school and on the course!

All my best,

John Ellett

JOHN F ELLETT

TABLE OF CONTENTS

INTRODUCTION

Congratulations! As a marketing leader embarking on a new mission this is an exciting time for you, one full of anticipation, excitement and, if you are like most of your peers, anxiety. You may be an experienced CMO taking on a new challenge, a first-time CMO who is ready to rise to the occasion or an aspiring CMO who wants to achieve career-accelerating success in your new position. You may be joining a new company or being promoted within your current firm. Whatever your circumstance, you want to get off to a fast start in your role and you know the first 100 days will be critical. You want to make great first impressions and you want to deliver on the expectations of the people who put you in your role.

This period is your unique window of opportunity to be the "newbie," to ask basic (yet insightful) questions, to challenge existing assumptions, to focus more on inputs than outputs and to take time simply to get to know other people in your organization. But that window won't be open for long. So how do you prioritize your activities to make the most of this unique period? You know the trajectory of your success will be established early in your tenure, so how can you accelerate your success, and that of your organization, through your initial actions?

These are the questions I have helped marketing executives answer over the years. I'd been in their shoes, had worked with many execs like them and had my own point of view, and yet I was curious to know if there was a "best practices" approach that I should be recommending.

I set out to see if I could deduce an approach by talking with over 50 CMOs and senior marketing executives about what they did in their first 100 days. As they told me what worked well and what they would like to do over, clear themes and patterns emerged. Those themes became the inspiration for the manifesto and the patterns became the structure for this book.

The overriding theme is that, as a new CMO (or marketing leader with another title), you have been hired to be a change agent. In some companies that means dramatic and disruptive change, impacting brand strategy, product plans, channel partners and communications programs. In others that means sustained and incremental change, focusing on executional improvements within the marketing organization. In all cases the changes impact strategy, execution, organizational structure, people, processes and systems. My research reinforced what you must already know: Your new assignment is not one dimensional. That is why the manifesto addresses so many facets of your role as change agent.

The patterns that emerged fall into three phases. The first is a preparation phase. It begins in the interview process and usually lasts about 30 days after starting the new job. It starts with getting clarity about the magnitude and pace of change your organization needs and what your executive team will support. It's followed by you translating those expectations into your agenda. It is important to distinguish your agenda from your strategy. While you are expected to show up with an idea of *how* you will solve the challenge you have been given, it is not wise to declare "the answer" on Day One. The strategy will follow in the next phase, but you'll need a clear agenda at the outset. You'll also need to build relationships with your executive peers and other key members of the company who will be important when it comes time to execute your eventual strategy. As with any leader of change initiatives, enrolling others in the process along the journey will make implementing your recommended changes easier when the time for action comes. Moving too fast and ignoring the human dynamics of change was a commonly requested "do-over" from several of the CMOs with whom I talked. Finally, you'll need to get the insights that will inform your strategy. These include "voice of the customer" insights, key market trends, competitive strengths and weaknesses and insights from within your own firm. Armed with clear expectations, a solid agenda, strong relationships and actionable insights, you can focus on the second phase of the process, the planning phase.

During this phase you'll develop your strategy, determine your organizational structure, make changes to your team roster and establish new processes by which the team will operate. These are the issues at the heart of your new role and you will want to address each of these carefully. The critical decisions you make in these four areas will ultimately impact your success. While you will be drawn quickly into day-to-day decisions assigned to your role, maintaining focus on the big picture decisions is essential. Which is why getting clarity on the pace of change is so critical in phase one. If you take too long to formalize the decisions around strategy and organization you may be viewed as a weak and ineffective leader, which will undermine your credibility. Conversely, if you act with too much haste before you have a clear picture, a sound strategy and organizational allies, you may be unsuccessful in the long run. Each situation is different, so make sure you get aligned with your boss and peers on the pacing of these decisions. For some CMOs all four of these areas were addressed in their first 100 days. For others it took six months given the culture and complexity of their companies. While the timing of this phase will vary, the sequence rarely does. The order — strategy, structure, people and process — is consistent and provides a framework around which you can order your key decisions. Once you have addressed these areas you can begin focusing on executing your strategy, the final phase of the process.

To execute your strategy you'll need a detailed action plan with responsible parties assigned to every activity. You'll want a measurement framework to assess progress toward your goals and to provide feedback for ongoing course correction and program optimization. You'll need technology-based systems to engage with your customers and partners and to improve the efficiency and effectiveness of your activities. And you'll need the executional agility to adjust your plans and programs based on the dynamic market and competitive environments within which you operate. These aspects of the last phase will likely extend beyond your first 100 days. Addressing each during your window of opportunity will enhance your ongoing effectiveness as a marketing leader.

Best of luck in your new opportunity. I hope the insights gleaned from other CMOs and shared on the following pages of this book will provide reassurance of your own instincts and possibly add a few new tools to your bag of tricks.

ACKNOWLEDGEMENTS

This book would not have been possible without the insights of CMOs and other marketing leaders who were generous with their time and gracious enough to introduce me to people I did not know. Some are quoted in the book, others are not, yet each person I talked with contributed something that shaped the structure and contents of the book.

Trying to write a book and run a company at the same time can be quite a challenge. I could not have undertaken this project without the support of the team at nFusion especially my partners Tom Martin and Jay Watson and my executive staff — Anne Spradley, Bill Parkes, Nikki Hickman and Bass Phillips.

As a rookie author, I could not have completed this manuscript without Britton Manasco who translated my ideas into an initial draft, Robi Polgar who edited my writing, Brad Langford who produced the graphics and Khoa Le who designed the cover.

Finally, I would not have had the confidence to undertake this effort without a lifetime of encouragement from my parents, my grandparents, my sister, my brother, my wife Terri and my sons Joe and Johnny. This book is dedicated to you.

THE CMO MANIFESTO

I'm not here to maintain the status quo but to be a leader of positive change for my organization.

I will bring focus where there is ambiguity, clarity where there is confusion and inspiration where there is doubt.

My ears will be open, my hand extended and my mind active. Trust will be built one relationship at a time. And we will succeed together.

The voice of the customer will be channeled through me and market insights will guide our decisions.

We can do anything, but we can't do everything, so we must be focused and intentional if we are to be great.

I will lead a high-performance team that will be accountable, agile and aligned.

My team can expect its teammates to be capable, committed and collaborative and the roster will change until those expectations are met.

We will find the right balance between chaos and stifling bureaucracy so that we can do remarkable things as efficiently as our business demands.

Our plan of action will have an emphasis on action.

We will embrace feedback, stay attuned to market dynamics, learn what works and optimize accordingly.

The latest in technology will not intimidate me but will pique my curiosity and provoke me to find innovative tools to enable sustainable progress.

By remaining resilient, responsible and relentless, we will prove the skeptics wrong and execute brilliantly in spite of the challenges we encounter.

And because of the courage of our conviction and the passion for our cause, we will make the future we envision.

I.

I'm not here to maintain the status quo but to be a leader of positive change for my organization.

CLARIFYING
EXPECTATIONS

When Jim Stengel was being considered for the role of CMO at Procter & Gamble in 2001, the company was in rough shape. The stock price had plunged. Market shares for key brands were not growing. People didn't have confidence in the company. If there had been a headline describing P&G it would have been, "It doesn't matter anymore."

But things were about to change. A new CEO, A.G. Lafley, had just been put in place and he was looking for a marketing leader who could help revitalize the 164-year-old firm. Stengel, an 18-year veteran of P&G, knew the company had a proud tradition of marketing leadership. Before he considered taking the job he wanted a clear idea about what it would take to be successful.

"Before my final meeting with A.G. I went out and talked with every living ex-CEO of P&G and asked them, 'What makes for an outstanding P&G CMO?' I talked to John Smale who was CEO in the '80s. I talked to Durk Jager. I talked to John Pepper. I talked to Ed Artz. I talked to a lot of the senior business leaders as well. Then I talked to some agency leaders. I wanted to know when the CMO is really in the zone."

In classic P&G style, Stengel then presented Lafley with a one-page memo stating how he would handle the new position. "We had a great dialogue," says Stengel. "He really liked what I was saying. He saw my passion for it. He saw the plan. We were highly aligned on the vision."

When Stengel took the position, one of his first actions was to put together a global marketing team. "Believe it or not, at P&G, there was never a global team," he says. "I went to all the major business units and I said, 'I would like you to loan me a person that you greatly respect who can be part of my team.'

"I put that team together. I got them feeling like they were a part of something terrific. That became the group through which we executed and refined the plan I had shown A.G. in my conversations with him."

So what enabled Stengel to get off to a strong start in his first 100 days? "I spoke to people," he says. "I traveled like crazy. I listened. I did some data gathering, time and motion studies. I looked at what people were working on. I found out what people valued. I talked to a lot of outsiders. Then I put my team together."

Once his team was in place, planning became critical: "I was real clear on what we were going to focus on, what success looked like and what the plan was. We continually refined it. We measured against it. We met monthly and, every month, we reviewed some area of the plan. We got into a rhythm and it really worked well."

Indeed it did. During Stengel's tenure sales doubled, profits quadrupled and P&G's market value increased by more than $100 billion. In his seven years as global marketing chief he led the transformation of P&G's marketing culture and reestablished the company as one of the most admired brands in the world.

CLARIFYING EXPECTATIONS SO YOU CAN MEET (AND EXCEED) THEM

Success as a marketing leader begins with expectations. Your challenge? That you fully understand and are aligned with the expectations of your senior management team.

The beginning of your journey as a new CMO is a moment of profound anticipation. The status quo is no longer acceptable and *you* — as the new marketing leader — are being brought in to lead some kind of change. The challenge up front is to ensure you are locked on to the overarching goals and objectives that are critical to your organization. It's vital that there is clear agreement on these expectations. Otherwise you are vulnerable to failure in your new role. If you aren't successful in meeting the expectations of others you are doomed to disappoint.

You can't afford to be out of sync with the rest of the leadership team. Should that happen you'll be trying to instigate change that the CEO or other members of the executive suite aren't prepared to support. In many cases this leads to organizational chaos. You end up trying to effect change that the business doesn't want to make. Or else you fail to produce the results that are expected of you.

That's why this first factor in the 100-day framework is so critical. This is the point where you align yourself with the individuals who are most essential to your achievement. The steps you take from this point must be consistent with the expectations of your core team. This is the only way to build trust and confidence. This is the only way to establish momentum and continue building it. And this is the only way to demonstrate that you have truly performed in line with the organization's mission and goals.

IT BEGINS DURING THE HIRING PROCESS

The clarification of expectations actually starts during the hiring process. This is where you have your first conversations with members of your team and, most important, your boss. You typically have an opportunity to ask probing and far-reaching questions that will give you a high-level perspective of the opportunities and challenges before you.

Indeed, it's important to maximize this chance to gain access and insight. You should reach out to the individuals who will have the greatest influence on your performance — and those whose perceptions of your performance matter most.

It's important to learn as much as you can at this point. One common mistake among those seeking new roles is being over-optimistic about the results they can deliver without knowing the obstacles they face or the resources that will be available to them.

While it may be tempting to reflect on past achievements and focus on selling your strengths, it's even more important to use this opportunity to learn the landscape. You need to know: What are the expectations? What kind of change is expected? Is the level of expected change transformational or incremental? What are the resources that will be available to effect change?

This is the time for determining whether the expectations of others are realistic and achievable. If not, it is necessary to refine or reset them. You are in a strong position to suggest — based on your experience — how existing goals might be made more achievable. If, in the end, you have the sense that you are being set up to fail, you'll want to politely step away and allow someone else to step into the role.

One marketing leader I interviewed learned this lesson the hard way when he took on the role of Marketing VP for a traditional manufacturing enterprise. He was hired to lead growth efforts for the large yet old-school company, which was newly intent on moving its business into electronic delivery systems that would serve small businesses. The VP was under the impression that his job was to help transform the enterprise — to reposition it for a new digital era. So he spent his first three months developing a new strategy, building a supporting organization and designing new operating processes. He believed he was on track to drive a successful business transformation effort.

But he soon learned that he wasn't on the same track as his CEO. The chief executive began asking for leads to support the company's online properties. It turned out that lead generation was at the center of his CEO's expectations. This was his measure of success for organizational improvement. Course correction proved impossible at this point and it wasn't long before the new VP stepped down. He says, in retrospect, he should have paid closer attention during the hiring process to the underlying concerns and measures that were motivating his boss. Having made initial assumptions that proved inaccurate (or insufficiently precise), he failed to meet expectations — leading to irresolvable conflict.

POST-ELECTION, PRE-INAUGURATION

But let's assume you accept the offer and the position. Congratulations. Much like the president-elect after an election, you'll typically have a brief transitional period leading up to the inauguration day — the day that you officially step into your new role. This is another opportunity for outreach. You have a chance to reach out to your colleagues on the senior management team as well as your direct reports — those you will be working with most actively in the marketing organization.

Some marketing leaders take advantage of this period to meet with team members on an informal basis — over coffee, lunch or perhaps a drink at the end of the day. It's a chance to get to know the people you'll be working with and begin building relationships.

In an informal and relaxed setting your colleagues might feel freer to share insights and perspectives, even war stories with you that are less likely to have been revealed during the hiring process. You also get a chance to relieve some of the stress and uncertainty that might accompany having a new colleague or boss.

KEY QUESTIONS TO CONFRONT AT THE OUTSET

At the outset of your first 100 days you need to raise a key set of questions that clarifies what is expected of you as comprehensively as possible. While there may be some distinctions from circumstance to circumstance, these questions are essentially the same no matter what your unique situation promises.

The responses you receive and the agreements you make early on must become your Polaris — the lodestar that provides guidance, clarity and inspiration as you navigate through your next set of challenges. In the absence of clarity you'll be liable to drift and perhaps lose your way. But if you ensure your key questions are answered fully, you will be well on your way to achieving impressive performance in your new role.

Question #1: What's the Overriding Goal I'm Expected to Accomplish?

The first question concerns goals and objectives. You want to know what you are expected to achieve or accomplish. You'll have lots of issues to manage once you get started but how do you make sure that the overriding goal is well understood?

Take David Roman, the CMO of Lenovo. Although business was reasonably strong, the Lenovo brand was lagging behind others in the consumer electronics sector. Roman was told he needed to build a brand that would take the business to new levels. Or consider David Ovens, the former CMO of Taco Bell. He was charged with developing a marketing strategy that would turn the business from negative growth to positive growth. The focus of his overriding goal was profitable growth.

Once you know and understand the overriding goal you are in a far stronger position to begin formulating the strategy that will help you achieve it. But don't just dive in. The purpose of addressing this question is to understand what the organization is trying to achieve. You don't need to know how you are going to achieve it at this point. You are being presented with a challenge. The solution for addressing it remains to be determined — and should be yours to decide.

Just be sure you fully understand the overriding goal as your executive colleagues see it. Ask them to elaborate as necessary to eliminate any ambiguities. Frustrations arise when clarity is not achieved around this first key question. When alignment is missing, paths will diverge. Marketing leaders will find themselves out of touch with the expectations of their executive colleagues — and lose credibility where they need it most.

Question #2: How Will My Success Be Measured in 100 Days? Six Months? One Year?

Your colleagues may be expecting you to develop a new branding initiative. Or they may be looking for a clear plan to generate leads and sales. They may even be expecting you to execute existing strategies and plans to produce quick wins.

Whatever the case, it's vital to be clear on milestones and measures of performance that are most important to your team. This will help you ensure you are taking the steps necessary to produce impressive results.

Fidelity's Chief Marketing Officer, Jim Speros, was able to capitalize on existing brand research and planning that had been done prior to his taking office. That allowed him to launch a new brand strategy and begin executing a campaign at the 100-day mark in his tenure. That's not the norm, however. More typical is the experience of Radio Shack's CMO Lee Applbaum. He was expected to develop a growth strategy and roadmap in his first 100 days. The supporting marketing campaigns would be executed in the months to follow.

What you are looking for is clarity about the pace of change. That's where the 100-day, 6-month and 12-month checkpoints come into play. Since most of a marketer's activities don't produce results overnight, you need to evaluate outcomes over time. You need to set particular milestones or timeframes and tie expected results to them.

Memories fade as time passes, so it's valuable to document expectations. A written agreement — or letter of understanding — can help keep all parties focused on the expectations that have been set and commitments that have been made. When it comes to accountability measures and milestones, it's best to eliminate as much ambiguity as possible.

I've spoken with several marketing executives who have been confronted with management dissatisfaction at a particular interval. However, they were able to respond by pointing to promised resources that had not yet been allocated. Their agreements strengthened their hands and justified their difficulties — even if their situations were not ideal.

There's clear power in the written word. If you haven't completed a letter of understanding in the hiring process then it's best to complete it in the first 30 days on the job. By ensuring you are in full agreement with your boss (and, perhaps, your executive colleagues) on the milestones that need to be reached and at what intervals, you set the stage for a far more productive relationship.

Question #3: What Is the Magnitude of Change I'm Expected to Lead?

There are various levels of change that you might be expected to lead. By understanding the magnitude as well as the rate of expected change, you ensure you are embarking on a change initiative that is consistent with the overriding goal of the organization.

Through research on *transformational alignment*, my firm, nFusion, has identified four distinct categories of change involving marketing leaders:

- **Business transformation.** This is a far-reaching change initiative concerned with determining what business an enterprise is in and how it will make money.
- **Brand transformation.** This approach is concerned with addressing the brand promise or value proposition and how it is expressed and delivered.
- **Organizational transformation.** This approach is focused on enhancing the marketing organization's structure, culture and

processes. Particular attention is focused on the people who will be on the team.

- **Executional transformation.** This approach revolves around the specific marketing programs and activities that must be deployed to produce results. Particular attention is focused on measuring results.

While the first two categories tend to be more strategic and expansive in nature, the latter two tend to be more tactical and incremental.

As an example of business transformation take Kodak, a company that was clearly struggling to determine what business it was in and to reposition itself for the future. The company, which was traditionally known for film and photography products, was challenged to make the transition to a dynamic, digital era. Jeffrey Hayzlett, the company's CMO during this critical transition, endeavored to help transform the business and enter new markets. As a result, the company developed a diversification strategy that it hoped would position it for survival and growth as the film business disappeared.

By contrast Fidelity's Speros and Radio Shack's Applbaum embarked on brand transformation initiatives. While they knew their businesses and what it took to make money, both their companies needed to become more relevant and compelling to the marketplace.

Erin Nelson, Dell's CMO until 2010, faced the challenge of organizational transformation. She was focused on effecting structural and process-related changes that would deliver greater results. She needed to rebuild confidence in marketing as a discipline and find the right balance between centralized corporate marketing and the teams aligned with individual business units.

A CMO facing the challenge of executional transformation was Colin Buechler, now CEO of LifeSize, a maker of high-definition videoconferencing solutions that had recently been purchased by peripherals giant, Logitech. While he was LifeSize's CMO, Buechler concentrated on the operational aspects of marketing, lead generation and sales enablement, helping the company meet its growth targets and compete with market challengers Cisco and Polycom.

Some marketing leaders will find themselves engaged in multiple categories of transformation at once. Indeed, executional transformation is likely to be vital for all firms eventually. It's just a question of priorities. As you lock on to the expectations of others in your executive team you'll have to clarify what type of transformation is most critical to address. Many other decisions — to be explored throughout this book — will flow from this one.

Question #4: What Resources (Human and Financial) Will Be Available to Me?

Without the resources necessary to drive change you are unlikely to be successful as a change leader. That's why it's necessary to clarify up front what human resources and financial resources will be available to support your efforts. You want to understand the budgeting process, how you will make requests and how you will justify those requests.

One marketing executive who worked with a large global electronics company told me about the conflicts that emerged as his leadership team sought results but refused to provide the funds necessary to launch new programs and campaigns. The company, which is well known for its consumer business, had ambitious growth targets in the business-to-business (BtoB) arena. He and his team created a multi-pronged strategy that revolved around enhancing the company's BtoB brand, put in place new marketing infrastructure and expanded the enterprise sales coverage model. But this marketing executive was stymied by a leadership team that was unwilling (or slow) to support him financially. When they asked him why he wasn't meeting expected growth targets, he was forced to point to an absence of resources — even though these resources had been promised to him at the outset of his efforts.

Such examples demonstrate why it's necessary to be careful what commitments you make early on and to ensure that you have real support — in terms of resources — to back up your change initiatives. Of course it's difficult (if not impossible) to be specific at the expectations stage as to the type and number of resources you will require. You will need to evaluate your situation over the next 30 – 60 days to formulate your strategy and plan. So your commitments at the outset should remain contingent on necessary resources being available to you. You can further clarify your commitments later on in the strategy and planning stages when you have a better sense of what resources — what talent and funds — will be available to you.

Question #5: Which Decisions Am I Expected to Make and Which Ones Am I Expected to Facilitate?

This is where the issue of decision rights and responsibilities comes into play. It's a question of which decisions are yours to make and which ones you can merely influence. You will have decisions on activities over which you have direct control, most of which will concern outcomes you are responsible for delivering. Other decisions may revolve around corporate mandates: Many of these decisions will affect others in the company who don't report to you. Social media policies — such as who can contribute commentary on blog sites — represent one example.

Finally there are decisions you don't make but over which you can exert an influence. In many companies it's necessary to lead by influence in order to encourage the sharing of best practices and methods. You may not have control over the budgets and policies of various business units, but you can encourage them to embrace strategies and approaches that have proven successful.

The CMO's responsibilities at Dr. Pepper/Snapple Group encompass brand strategy, advertising, customer insights and product innovation with direct control over many decisions. A company such as Samsung, however, is highly decentralized, requiring the CMO to devote a lot of energy to leading by influence. The CMO there is challenged to introduce smart new marketing approaches while respecting the decision-making authority of the firm's various business unit leaders, who must be enlisted to support the CMO's initiatives.

Question #6: How Will I Interact with My Boss?

Don't underestimate this issue. One of the keys to getting the support you need is keeping your boss enrolled. For your individual success, how well you are supported by your boss comes down to how well you interact with him or her.

You need to know a few things: What's your boss's style? How should information be presented? How will the two of you communicate? When will you meet? Does he or she want to be actively briefed on your decisions and progress or is it preferable just to present updates on certain milestones and initiatives?

Some marketing leaders I interviewed for this book expressed that their bosses — typically CEOs — prefer intimate detail and exhaustive reviews. They want to be fully apprised of the progress being made in the marketing organization. Yet other marketing leaders describe bosses who prefer strategic conversations and high-level reports at agreed-upon intervals. They aren't interested in getting bogged down in extensive detail. They just want to be certain that their marketing leaders are on a path to successful outcomes.

Whatever the case in your situation, you have to be in sync with your boss and communicate effectively. This is essential if you are to build trust and establish the confidence necessary to win top-level support.

COMMON MISTAKES TO AVOID

Marketing leaders sometimes make mistakes that can undermine their success at the outset of their new appointments. One is the tendency to make changes they think are part of their mandate that, ultimately, the organization isn't committed to making. In this situation the new CMO's desired changes are out of sync with changes anticipated by the CEO and other members of the leadership team. There are limits, after all, to the amount of disruptive change an organization is likely to accept.

The second mistake is to believe that you have more control than you really do. You have to recognize what decisions you own and which ones you can merely influence. What are the big things that everyone agrees need to be done? Mistakes are made when the marketing leader has a different viewpoint on this matter than the other key leaders in the organization.

The third mistake is making expansive commitments about what you can accomplish before you understand the resources that will be available to you and the amount of change the organizational culture can accept. That will lead to frustration and disappointment. You would be over-committing without knowing the constraints you are dealing with. It's hard to walk back commitments you've already made.

But not to worry: If you are diligent at the outset in terms of clarifying the expectations of others (and most particularly the members of your senior management team), you are in a great position to move on to the challenge of setting an agenda that will lead to impressive results. We'll address this in the next chapter.

ACTION PLAN CHECKLIST

1. State your primary goal in one sentence.
2. Articulate at least one tangible measure of success for:

   a) Your first 100 days
   b) Your first six months
   c) Your first year

3. Describe in one short paragraph the nature of the change you will be leading and why the status quo is no longer acceptable.
4. Schedule a recurring meeting with your boss and agree on standard discussion topics.

II.

I will bring focus where there is ambiguity, clarity where there is confusion and inspiration where there is doubt.

SETTING YOUR AGENDA

It was two weeks before Andy England was to step into his new role as CMO of Coors Brewing when he had a conversation of extreme consequence.

"I inherited an assistant who had worked with a series of CMOs before I showed up," he says. "I think she worked with three or four CMOs before me. As you know, the CMO position can be a revolving door. Anyway, she was very eager to get started, very conscientious if you like. She said she'd organize a meeting with the marketing department. Then she said something which I thought was both a little precocious and also intimidating: 'You should probably use that opportunity to explain your marketing philosophy.'"

England now says it was the best advice he could have possibly received at that point. As he explains it, "I spent quite of bit of time actually pondering what I wanted to tell people about my marketing philosophy on Day One. What do I believe in? It wasn't that I didn't believe in things. I just hadn't committed them to paper or a PowerPoint deck. I spent quite a bit of time actually putting my thoughts down in a deck that only had a few words on each slide. The thought that stuck with people more than any other was this: 'Great marketers take complex situations and distill simple and actionable truths.'"

By taking time to articulate his marketing philosophy and then share it with his organization, England helped his team quickly learn what was important to him and therefore how they could meet his expectations effectively.

SETTING AND ARTICULATING YOUR AGENDA

All eyes are on you, the newly appointed marketing leader. People throughout the organization are waiting to see how you'll present yourself and set the tone for what's next.

While your boss and some of your colleagues should have received a strong sense of your character and perspectives in the hiring process, there are others — most especially those reporting to you — who may still be anxious to know who you are as a person. They want to know what you are going to do in your new role. What actions will you take?

This is the point at which you must set and articulate your agenda. While your first challenge was to learn the expectations of others, your challenge now is to begin to set expectations for your team.

You are now engaged in a process of answering their questions: Who are you? What are you going to do? How much change are you going to make? What's your basic timetable for the key actions you're going to take? How should team members work with you? What decisions do you need to be involved in up front? Which ones are you going to defer? Do you like lots of detail or do you prefer summary information from those reporting to you?

Indeed, you can think of your agenda in terms of addressing a specific set of questions. By answering them you will begin creating trust and confidence — with your executive colleagues, your direct reports and your marketing organization overall.

Remember, the people around you are deeply concerned about and interested in the changes you will undertake. Your actions will have implications for their careers. Some may even be concerned that their jobs are on the line — and their concerns may be justified. Most will be seeking reassurance that their new leader is capable of taking them to new levels of success.

It's important to act fast. You should begin developing your agenda in the transition period between accepting the position and stepping into it. The first day you actually step into the role people will be forming impressions and making assumptions. It's best that you seize the moment and ensure those impressions are the ones you want to make. You want to demonstrate that you are an active and able leader. You want to show that you're prepared for the challenge ahead.

When you roll out your agenda, present it in a sequence. First, present to your boss and peers. Make sure you have confirmation from them — and that your agenda reflects what has been discussed previously. Then you can present your agenda more widely. Your direct reports will come next and, finally, the wider marketing organization. The forum (or medium) for that presentation will depend on what's the best way to reach your people, but the point is that everyone will be anxious to know what you plan to do.

As with the sample agenda that follows, you should lay out the key milestones you intend to address along a timeline. This will help all parties mentally prepare for the challenge ahead. By defining your expectations in this vivid way you will provide clarity and light the path forward.

Sample First 100 Days Agenda

	Month 1	Month 2	Month 3	Month 4
Meet with peers, team and franchise partners	■			
Gather insights to inform strategy	■	■		
Develop revised brand strategy	■	■		
Modify marketing organization		■	■	
Refine operating processes		■	■	
Revamp marketing plan		■	■	
Engage employees and franchise partners in embracing new plan			■	■
Establish operating metrics and reviews			■	■
Invest in key marketing systems				■

So what issues must you address at the start of your tenure to set others' expectations? The following are some items to incorporate into your agenda for success.

Agenda Item #1: Your Principles of Success

Perhaps the most important thing you can do when introducing yourself to your new team is to articulate your principles of success, including who you are and what you believe. There are many ways to do this. For Andy England it was a presentation that laid out his marketing philosophy to his new team. Peter Horst, Senior Vice President of Marketing at Capital One Bank, published his principles in his first month on the job. His four tenets were simply stated yet powerful if followed. Horst insisted on:

1. **Clear accountability.** Be 100 percent aligned with clients' business goals and priorities; share the successes, yet have clear accountabilities; be transparent in your actions.

2. **Brilliant execution**. Always be on time, on budget, on strategy, on brand; be highly coordinated and totally aligned; set clear expectations and deliver on them consistently with efficient processes and rapid response.

3. **Bold moves**. Bring new and provocative thinking with a clear, strong point of view; continuously test bold hypotheses and make major impacts on the business.

4. **Seamless collaboration**. Act as one company, one team and with one outcome; have each others' backs; engage in candid dialogue and constructive, yet respectful conflict; no drama, no intrigue, no in-fighting, none!

I was particularly struck by that last point. Creating a culture of "no drama, no intrigue and no in-fighting" is not easy, especially in large companies in challenging industries. It starts at the top by declaring a zero-tolerance policy and then reinforcing it with actions on a daily basis. Yet, in the end, this creates an environment that is not only more fun, but that allows the company to operate better.

There are many ways to express who you are and what you believe. The key is to find a way that is appropriate to you. Your peers and team members are trying to get a grasp of your character and what matters most to you. They'd like to understand your values and hear your personal mission statement. This will help them understand who you are as a leader.

Agenda Item #2: What You Intend to Accomplish

Having introduced yourself and your principles of success to your team, now is the time to articulate your overriding goal — the expectations clarified in your initial process of discovery. You have aligned on what your boss and your senior-level colleagues expect you to accomplish; now it's necessary to communicate this charter more widely to your direct reports and the rest of the marketing organization.

Of course, the executive team is eager to know that you've heard and understood its expectations. The way you articulate your high-level charter is the first step in ensuring that you are aligned with the executive team's agenda.

You can provide a uniting focus for all parties by boldly stating what needs to be achieved. The more clearly you can articulate your goals, objectives and aspirations, the better. This helps to ensure that everyone is moving in the same direction from the beginning.

David Ovens was clear about two things when he arrived in his new position at Taco Bell. The first was his overriding goal to return the brand to consistent, profitable growth. The second was that he and his team had two months before the annual franchisee meeting to develop a plan that would inspire confidence among this important constituency. With a sense of clarity and urgency he marshaled the internal and external resources needed to refocus the brand to be a value leader in the quick-serve restaurant category.

Agenda Item #3: The Type, Magnitude and Pace of Change You Will Be Leading

As with the overriding goal, your explanation of the change ahead will be shaped by your prior conversations about expectations. Everyone expects change of some sort. Now it's time to tell your team what sort of change is coming. Will it address the business? The brand? The organization? Operational processes?

The nature of the change to come will require some elaboration. You'll need to explain in greater depth what this type of change will involve and why it is necessary.

People in the organization will want to know how big the change will be. Will it be transformational or incremental? Jeffrey Hayzlett needed to help transform Kodak's dependency on a dying film business by diversifying aggressively into new categories. There was a clear understanding that the company was standing on a "burning platform." David Roman's charter at Lenovo was centered around brand transformation. "I was asked to develop the brand at the same pace as the business," he says.

Your team will want to know the timeframes for this change. What are the key milestones ahead and when must they be met? Key milestones can take many forms. Jim Speros had much of the spadework completed before he arrived as CMO at Fidelity so he could focus on launching and executing a transformational brand strategy within his first 100 days. David Roman, however, needed the first 100 days at Lenovo to develop his marketing proposal for the executive team to endorse. He needed input and validation from important constituents for the strategy itself, but execution would come during his second 100 days.

Agenda Item #4: How You Expect to Work with Your Peers and Your Organization

So much of success is tied to personal relationships and interactions. Executives who hope to succeed must learn to manage interpersonal relationships, investing time and effort in the individuals who are essential to effective outcomes.

You want to clarify when and how you are going to meet with your executive peers and your direct reports. You want to consider several questions:

- Who are you?
- What issues do you wish to address with your executive peers and your direct reports?
- How are you going to make decisions together?
- Where will you meet and when?

When Nigel Dessau started in his role as CMO for AMD he wanted to model transparency to his team: "I told my people who I am, my history, my Myers-Briggs result — and that's all I did for 15 minutes. I actually put that deck together to say, 'Here's my family, my wife, me, how I grew up. Here's how I think, here's what I think about and this is what I'm interested in. As for what my objectives are, I am just going to listen for the next 30 days.' I don't think anyone had ever done that before at AMD as a new leader. They all walked away knowing something more about me besides that I was the new boss."

Because an organization is comprised of multiple disciplines, you need to be able to communicate to individuals in ways that indicate that you understand their various roles and responsibilities and that you are eager to work with them. When meeting with the chief financial officer you'll want to explore how budgeting is going to work. What's necessary to justify budgets and make the case for key investments? When meeting with the head of sales it's critical to explore how to align marketing with the sales function. When meeting with product development you want to focus on what role marketing can play to create more innovative and relevant products. Conversations that build relationships are essential to success. Your job when rolling out your agenda is to set the stage for interactions with your peers and team members that will produce compelling outcomes. You need to clarify how you are going to collaborate effectively.

Agenda Item #5: The Decisions You'll Make (and Defer) in Your First 100 Days

To keep everyone focused on what's important you'll want to clarify the decisions you will be making in the first 100 days as well as the decisions that will be deferred. It's easy, after all, to get distracted by all the possible concerns that might arise in this period. That's why you'll want to draw some distinct lines.

Radio Shack CMO Lee Applbaum stepped into his role with a laser focus on making the brand relevant again. He stated up front that he would be focused on making decisions concerned with the brand's future strategy in his first 100 days. As such he allowed existing approaches regarding advertising and marketing campaigns to remain in place. He would defer or delegate decisions regarding retail marketing strategy. He recognized that there was only marginal value in making incremental changes in retail approaches early on when a brand transformation would influence those approaches over time. He wanted to keep his eye on the brand itself.

However, sometimes it's not so easy to delineate which decisions should get made in the first 100 days and which should not. When there is ambiguity of this sort it may make sense to set up decision forums involving your direct reports and other relevant parties. These forums can provide a place for reviewing decision-making concerns and clarifying priorities as you go.

Agenda Item #6: Your Expectations of Your Team

Your marketing team will be particularly eager to learn what you expect of them. This is your opportunity to break down your agenda in terms of what will happen in the next 100 days and what you expect them to accomplish, individually and as a group. What are their roles and responsibilities?

One marketing executive at a major technology company made the mistake early on of insulting his inherited marketing organization in a major business publication. His intent was to set the stage for change by pointing out some of the limitations of his company's prior marketing efforts. Unfortunately, he ended up alienating his team at the start of the relationship. They took his on-the-record comments, which suggested that they were professionally incompetent, as an insult. Unsurprisingly, he didn't last long in his executive role.

Rather, you'll want to pull aside your various marketing groups — whether it's your advertising, channels or market intelligence teams — and provide reasonably specific assignments. Let them know what you are looking for and how you expect to receive it. How do they keep you apprised of progress? How should they provide reports and at what intervals?

The CMO from Motorola Mobility, Bill Ogle, asked each one of his direct reports to prepare for him an evaluation of what was working, what was not working and what needed improvement. This exercise helped give him greater clarity in terms of what his priorities should be and where, as a leader, he could most effectively add value. It also gave him a stronger sense of the caliber of his team — whom he could count on as the challenges began to mount.

Agenda Item #7: Your Hypothesis for a Winning Strategy

Working with your team to collect data and insight, you will spend a good portion of your first month or so focused on developing a hypothesis for a successful strategy. You'll want to test elements of your hypothesis on trusted peers and team members, but you won't want to reveal all of it too early in your tenure. It should remain undisclosed early on.

Some marketing leaders make the mistake of thinking they have to declare a grand strategy at the outset. They want to capture the attention of their people and motivate them. They want to make a big splash and establish a sense of urgency.

The problem with revealing too much too early is that you have not proven yourself. If you unveil your strategy too early the people around you will rightly think that you've jumped the gun. "You just got here," they'll think. "How could you have all the answers already?" Naturally your credibility will diminish. Your team members are expecting you to struggle with the questions before providing appropriate answers.

That said, you don't want to show up and appear to be aimless. You want to have a well informed hypothesis based on what you learned through your prior interviews and research. You're not coming into the situation completely cold. In fact, you may have a pretty good grasp of the issues and a strong sense of what needs to be done, especially if you've transferred into the role from somewhere else in the company. But, one way or another, you should be developing a hypothesis that you can test and validate going forward — even if it's not (and shouldn't be) explicitly stated. This hypothesis can guide your next round of discovery — the conversations, investigations and analysis that will ultimately lead to your marketing strategy.

Jim Stengel put together a one-pager on his proposed plan for P&G and previewed it with his CEO. "During my first 100 days, I wanted to come out of the blocks very fast on what I believed in without being specific on the plan. I didn't want to come out and broadcast to the organization the one-pager I'd shared with [CEO] A.G. [Lafley] because it just wasn't the right thing to do. But I wanted to come out with who I am, what I believe in, what I value and generally where I'll be focusing."

As we'll discuss later in the book, you will eventually reveal your strategy and then your plan for achieving it. But for now you don't want to reveal too much. Just let your hypothesis sharpen your exploration of your new surroundings. Test it. Refine it. Strengthen it. Let it help you focus and prioritize. Don't reveal your hypothesis until the time is right.

DAY ONE IN YOUR NEW POSITION

There is always a Day One — and it's interesting to see how different marketing leaders spend this first day. Some spend half the day tied up with the human resources people filling out paperwork. At some point, however, you will step into your new office and everyone around you will be wondering what you'll do next.

It's important to prepare for this first day. You want to make the right first impression. You'll want to hit the ground running in terms of introducing your agenda — as opposed to your strategy — to your immediate team and, then, to the wider marketing organization.

From the start there will be questions that your people are looking to you to answer. You'll want to give your answers thoughtful consideration beforehand. You're signaling where you intend to take them on the journey ahead. Seize the moment. Be candid about who you are and what you expect. Address the key items on your agenda.

When Jim Stengel started his job at Procter & Gamble, he decided one of the first things he would do is introduce himself — via webcast — to marketing employees around the world. "I basically told stories," he explains. "P&G has been at its best in its history when it was seen as the best marketing company in the world. I said, 'There's no reason we can't recapture that. No reason whatsoever.'"

His team members responded positively. "People got onboard," he says. "'What do I do? Where do we start? How can I be a part of this?' That's what I heard. I was frankly overwhelmed by people saying, 'I want to help.'"

Just remember: It's a highly charged moment and there will be a heightened state of awareness. There will be a certain amount of trepidation, anticipation and hopefulness. Your team wants to trust you. They want to believe in you. They want to know that you are acting in the company's best interests and in their best interests. This is your chance to win them over.

ACTION PLAN CHECKLIST

1. Prepare a "top 10 list" presentation that addresses these questions:

   a) Who are you?
   b) Why are you here?
   c) What kind of change initiative are you leading?
   d) What do you believe about marketing?
   e) What do you value?
   f) How do you like to work with others?
   g) What are your top priorities?
   h) What are key milestones for your first six months?
   i) What do you expect from your team?
   j) What can they expect from you?

2. Schedule the following meetings:

   a) Hypothesis review with your boss
   b) Direct reports meeting or series of one-on-one meetings to review your top 10 list
   c) All-hands department meeting to review your top 10 list

III.

My ears will be open, my hand extended and my mind active. Trust will be built one relationship at a time. And we will succeed together.

FORGING
RELATIONSHIPS

As Chris Hummel prepared to become the CMO of Siemens Enterprise Communications his enthusiasm for the challenge ahead grew. "The reason I took the role was because it was positioned as a change agent for the company. So I asked myself, 'Can I really impact this company? Not just the marketing function but the whole company.' Obviously the CMO can change the marketing strategy and the marketing approach, but can he really have an impact on the company and therefore actually have an impact on his industry?" So with the conviction he could help transform the company, Hummel set about his quest.

"The difference between a successful CMO and an okay CMO in all my experience having watched bosses, peers, my own roles, is the ability to set the agenda versus having the agenda set for you. And it's hard to do. So the way that I went about it was to build relationships with my peers. Not just with my boss, but with the other people on the C-suite. I wanted to understand their agendas, to be able to translate their agendas into the good of the company, into my own selfish needs and to find a way to actually serve the people who take the ball.

"I found that the engineering and product teams understood they both needed each other but they didn't really know how to talk to each other. So I started to facilitate relationships between both and acted to some degree as a translator. If you can act as a facilitator of that kind of collaboration between members of the C-suite, you become indispensible and you also gain the intelligence necessary to do your job. So that was one of the big things I focused on.

"That was the only way I was going to be able to figure out how to scope quick and early signature wins. Because whether it's your first 10 days or 50 days or 100 days or whatever it is, if by that point you don't have some signature wins, something that you can put your stamp on, you're probably getting pressed into, 'My website's not up,' 'I have to run events,' 'What's happening over here,' and then you're in pure firefighting mode. So it's strong peer relationships that helped me to understand what's going on in the rest of the business, to help identify what the scope of the role could be and where I could carve out the most impactful space. That was personally challenging and, importantly, delivered some value to the business."

BUILDING RELATIONSHIPS TO DRIVE CHANGE

Change is not something that a new market leader can simply demand or mandate. To effect change successfully you must engage key allies and encourage others to participate in a new approach. You must enroll people in the process rather than dictate to them. This is why relationship building is another important factor in the foundation of success.

One of the most compelling aspects of the marketing function is that it has a considerable impact on just about every other function within the organization, particularly if the marketing team is charged with driving growth. So, if you are going to be a successful marketing leader who inspires and leads change you must build relationships across the enterprise.

Relationship building with executive peers is especially important. These are the individuals who are most influential in terms of supporting and evaluating your performance. You'll be accountable to them. You'll also need them on board and engaged when you eventually reveal your strategy and plan for meeting your overriding goals and objectives. You'll need their shared commitment to your initiatives.

Let's consider the individuals on the senior management team — the C-suite — and why these relationships are important.

- **The CEO.** Most CMOs report directly to the chief executive. This individual is responsible for the overall strategy of the firm and for delivering value to shareholders. Hopefully, you will collaborate closely with the CEO to roll out a growth strategy that inspires the entire organization. The CEO will be looking to you to provide insights on market trends and customer demands that will help to propel the organization forward. The most important issue in this relationship is aligning on the nature of change that's expected — just as P&G's Jim Stengel and A.G. Lafley did with spectacular results.
- **The CFO.** The chief financial officer oversees funding for all major initiatives and is responsible for the enterprise's financial management. This person will be essential if you are to obtain the financial and human resources necessary to meet your objectives. You'll need to learn the language of finance to justify your budget requests convincingly and provide credible performance reports. The key here is to align on financial goals such as profit and growth as well as softer measures such as those tied to brand.
- **The CRO.** The chief revenue officer (who may very well have another title) is the person responsible for generating sales in the field. This person is looking to you to attract new prospects to the organization, strengthen existing customer relationships and set the stage for new sales opportunities. Alignment here — which is often difficult to obtain — is essential to revenue

growth. The CRO must close the deals you set up. What's critical here is to align on the ideal customer, the value proposition and short-term measures of success as they may apply to various segments or product units.

- **The CIO.** The chief information officer is increasingly vital to the success of marketing. Given the proliferating number of channels that depend on new technology (such as the Web, eCRM and social networking), you must collaborate with the CIO to ensure you have the marketing infrastructure to conduct campaigns. Varying forms of marketing automation, meanwhile, will enhance your efficiency and effectiveness.

- **The CPO.** Whoever holds the top job in human resources can be considered the chief people officer. This person will be vital in terms of obtaining the talent you need to execute ambitious plans — and to see that your people are properly motivated. The CPO will help you structure compensation and professional development plans so that your people are fully engaged. Without the right talent and the right motivations you are unlikely to create a marketing organization that can consistently deliver solid results.

- **The CTO.** The leader of product innovation and development is known by different monikers, for example, chief technology officer, head of culinary innovation or SVP of product development. Regardless of the title, assuring the products you bring to market will meet customer needs is going to be the key to your success. So building a strong alliance with your product development team is essential.

The next set of relationships that matter to your success exists within your marketing organization. It is particularly critical that you cultivate a dynamic group of lieutenants — your direct reports — to provide insight and help you execute your marketing strategies.

Marketing organizations take many forms. You may have teams responsible for product marketing, marketing communications, brand strategy, field marketing, market research and various channels. Your structure, to some extent, will depend on your industry or the way your enterprise goes to market.

While you will rely on your direct reports to manage and motivate their people, you will be expected to provide overarching guidance and inspiration. This is what it means to be a leader. You set the tone. The priorities and principles you establish with your immediate circle — your marketing team — are likely to be reflected within the marketing organization as a whole.

Still other relationships that matter might include your agency and consulting partners — whether they are responsible for advertising, direct marketing, interactive media, social media, public relations or some other set of services. You'll need to collaborate with these partners to develop smart strategies and execute them as effectively as possible. Many companies do a poor job of managing their agency relationships, minimizing their results in the marketplace. To ensure success you'll want to seek out reliable guidance and advice based on proven results. Indeed, an independent advisor can be critical at this stage — providing a candid and neutral perspective as you formulate your strategy.

Some marketing leaders are responsible for managing their distribution, franchise and external channel partnerships. These partners play a customer-facing role in your organizational ecosystem. They represent your brand and deliver the final experience to your customers. They possess perspectives and insights that are essential to your ability to operate. You'll need to determine how best to engage these partners and facilitate their success.

COLLABORATION FOR SUPERIOR RESULTS

Research has shown that collaborative organizations tend to generate superior results over time. But building a collaborative team is not easy. At nFusion we've developed a model to provide guidance when considering the actions to take to build collaboration and achieve objectives.

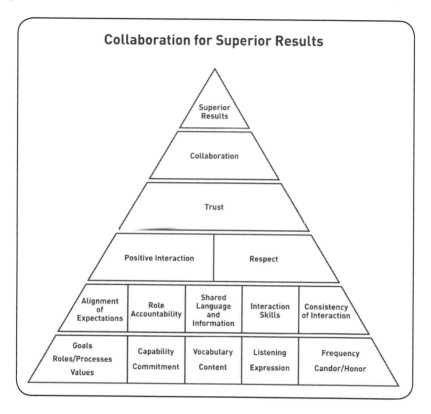

To understand this model start at the top, the apex of the pyramid, and work your way down. The assumption here is that a collaborative organization can deliver better results. Whether this is collaboration within a single enterprise or several, the point is that you must reach across boundaries and seek out mutual ground if you are to reach new levels of performance. Otherwise you end up with fragmented fiefdoms — and this can be deeply problematic. David Aaker's recent book, *Spanning Silos – The New CMO Imperative*, explains this well.

When organizations split into silos they are less likely to share data, for instance. Product groups are famous for protecting their customer data, making it impossible for a marketing organization to produce a single, unified view of the customer — a critical step when trying to determine the real value (or potential value) of your individual customers and evaluate how you can address them most effectively.

Sales and marketing organizations can find themselves at odds. Marketing might contend that sales is failing to follow up on the leads it has generated, while sales will complain that the leads are of little worth. Finger pointing ensues, making failure inevitable.

One marketing leader I interviewed told the story of how his company sought global growth for its technology products, yet failed to recognize how limited its sales coverage model was in distant countries. This led to constant clashes between marketing and sales. Had marketing, sales and the company's executive leaders created a better dialogue it might have been easier to identify these gaps in the global sales coverage model and avoid the inevitable conflicts that emerged.

Collaboration is often quite taxing and difficult. To make it work, you have to cultivate trust.

Trust, in fact, is at the core of this collaboration model. In the absence of trust, effective collaboration will be hard to attain. No one will want to share information or best practices. There will be no effort to embrace joint accountability for outcomes.

Trust, for its part, depends on having positive interactions and mutual respect for other parties. Through the continuous sharing of insights and a joint commitment to results, you begin to see the world through the eyes of your counterparts. You become increasingly unified. You also become far more honest and open.

One of the misconceptions about collaboration is that it means an absence of arguments, disagreements or conflict. Nothing could be further from the truth. As trust builds you can openly address difficult issues and acknowledge points of disagreement. You can debate the hard issues, accept disagreement and not walk away wounded. Your goal is to surface the best thinking in people — their outspoken opinions and insights. By sharing your candid thoughts and perspectives in a respectful way you can come to better conclusions and outcomes. To have these types of conversations, however, there must be a foundation of trust.

One executive with whom I'm familiar came into his role seeking to develop a strong relationship with the CEO, but proceeded to alienate the business unit leaders that would be responsible for executing new marketing approaches. By boorishly attempting to centralize power and making a land grab for marketing resources he made it impossible to establish trust.

However, another marketing executive I know — Nancy Hampton, CMO at CiCi's Pizza, who previously ran brand marketing for Macaroni Grill — showed how trust could be built effectively. While at Macaroni Grill she was charged with leading marketing efforts as the company was being split off from and sold by its parent. By creating a strong bond with her leadership team she helped establish an environment that the acquiring company wanted to maintain. As a result, key leadership team members — including Hampton, the CFO, the COO and the head of human resources — remained intact as a team for some time after the sale. They had developed a high degree of trust and mutual respect.

THE ELEMENTS OF SMART COLLABORATION

It's important to recognize that you can't just say "Trust people" and assume it will happen. That's why the issue of relationship building must be addressed carefully in your first 30 days. You'll want to start with the foundational elements that contribute to relationship building, shown at the base of the pyramid. These elements represent the building blocks that go into creating a collaborative, high-performing organization. Among them:

Alignment of Expectations. This element begins with creating common goals. When I was running the North American marketing organization at Dell I ran into conflicts with the vice president of manufacturing. I was trying to build more customer options into our products to generate demand. After all, I was evaluated on how much demand I could produce. He was trying to reduce the number of options — reducing complexity — because his bonus was based on inventory turns. The fewer options the easier it would be for him to meet his objective.

Once we understood that the company had important goals that were in conflict we were able to find ways to mitigate each other's issues. When goals are misaligned the ability to collaborate and build relationships is undermined. A sales leader, whose goal is quarterly revenue, and a marketing leader, whose goal is changes in brand reputation, could easily find themselves at odds.

You must engage in processes that are consistent across differing groups. Marketing and R&D, for instance, must work together to define a product in consistent ways. They need to be fundamentally aligned on values — and seek common ground where there is a divergence. You want to know how you can add value for your peers. What do they expect from you?

Role Accountability. It's one thing to agree on roles and goals. It's another thing to deliver on expectations. This element comes into play as you begin to determine whether you have the right resources and capabilities to meet required roles. Does your organization have the right kind of people, the necessary funding and the organizational capability to fill necessary roles? Is there commitment, on an individual level, to achieving established goals?

One large company my agency worked with was attempting to build a new marketing communications group. Unfortunately, other groups were withholding the support and information necessary to make this new marcom team successful. In order to protect their turf, other groups were willing to sabotage the new team. Clearly there was no commitment to fulfilling the roles necessary for mutual success.

Shared Language and Information. Yet another consequential element of relationship building is the ability to establish a shared language.

This is why industry experience is often a requirement. If you are new to a business or product category, you'll want to immerse yourself in the language that matters to the enterprise. You may be confronted with all sorts of acronyms and technical jargon. Take advantage of the early days in your role to ask for clarity when you're uncertain of what something means.

Consider the relationship between marketing and finance. Finance works with numbers on a constant basis. It evaluates funding decisions based on factors such as return on investment, payback period and net present value. Finance leaders are less concerned about measures that are popular in marketing circles — measures of brand awareness, advertising coverage or website traffic. The challenge is to come together on quantifiable terms that will resonate with both parties. The medium is also important. If you hope to influence finance you'll want to become deeply conversant with the presentation of spreadsheets.

Take Walgreens CMO Kim Feil. As the first individual to hold that title at the company she focused on communicating how marketing would be accountable for clear and measurable results. This enabled the company's CFO and other executive peers actively to track her organization's progress in a language that was clear to them. She broke down her progress reports into short-term, medium-term and long-term projections. This system of measures proved to be a powerful way for her to build trust in a new role with the people whose support she most needed to cultivate.

By establishing a shared vocabulary and context for conversations you set the stage for deeper engagement and greater confidence. Too often worlds become unbridgeable when there is no way to share information and insight effectively. By addressing this challenge up front you are well on your way to establishing trust.

Interaction Skills. If you are to be successful collaborating and building relationships with your team you'll need to be a strong communicator. One of the most important skills to accomplish this is active listening. It is especially critical during your first 30 days to ask probing and thoughtful questions that help you understand the goals, needs and perspectives of others. Not only are you learning what must happen to achieve success, you are demonstrating interest in the concerns of others.

It comes down to how you express yourself. Are you coming off as someone who expects to force his or her will on others and lead through intimidation or are you coming off as a leader who genuinely cares about the contributions of the team and is prepared to lead through engagement? Are you bullying others into submission or winning them over to your side?

Consistency of Interaction. The last element to successful collaboration is the consistency with which you interact with others. This is partially related to frequency of interaction. You can't engage others if you are rarely reaching out to them. It's also a matter of candor and honesty. Are you willing and able to have difficult conversations in an open and respectful way?

If you reach out to your people on a consistent and frequent basis you'll help to create a more predictable and trustful environment. The CEO of Miller Coors, for example, demanded that Andy England and the other members of the C-suite officed on the same floor to ensure a high frequency of informal interaction.

When you are erratic or unpredictable you are, by contrast, likely to make honest communication and collaboration more difficult. It's best simply to set expectations and meet them with respect to how you want to communicate. By candidly sharing your thoughts and perspectives in these interactions you'll invite others to reciprocate.

CHARACTER BUILDS CONFIDENCE

So much of success in relationship building comes down to character. It's a subject I had the privilege of discussing with Doug Brooks, CEO of Brinker International, parent company of Chili's Grill & Bar and Maggiano's Little Italy restaurants. My agency has worked with Brooks' team on a variety of interactive projects.

The conversation was prompted by my attendance at the annual gala for Limbs for Life, a fundraiser for an organization that provides artificial limbs for those who would otherwise be without, for which Brooks serves as both a board member and event co-chair.

I asked him about the importance of character in being an effective leader in both the for-profit and not-for-profit worlds. He is quite passionate about the subject and shared some of the wisdom he gained from his mentors.

On Respect: "My first job was as a dishwasher in a fried chicken restaurant when I was 13. I had two managers, Mike and Bob, whose different styles made quite an impression on me at an early age. Mike would look me in the eye, call me by name and say things like 'Doug, nice job on the dishes today.' On the other hand, Bob would yell across the kitchen, 'Hey you, you missed a spot.' That experience has stuck with me for over 40 years. I learned a lot about respect: If you give it, you'll get it."

On Honesty: "It is important for me to give my team members honest feedback because I care. I'm on their side and I want them to be better."

On Leaders: "We once had Lou Holtz, former head coach of Notre Dame football, talk to a group of Chili's managers. He said there were three questions he expected all of his players to be able to answer affirmatively about him as their leader. Can I trust you? Do you care about me? Do you want to win (do you share my goals)?"

On Courage: "When I lost my leg in 1998, I had to decide if it was going to be an excuse to feel sorry for myself. Some things you just can't control. Lack of character leads to excuses."

On Being a Role Model: "The way I behave sets the tone."

One other attribute that Brooks did not talk about was humility. He doesn't like to talk about himself and rarely grants interviews. But Brooks is a humble leader and that has endeared him even more to those who have got to know him.

His example is relevant for all marketing leaders. Give respect and you'll receive it. Show you care and great care will be taken. Trust others and they will trust you.

ACTION PLAN CHECKLIST

1. List your most important peer relationships.

   a) Who are they?
   b) What are their career histories and experience at your firm?
   c) What are their most important measures of success?
   d) What do you expect from them?
   e) What do they expect from you?
   f) Do you have regularly scheduled meeting times?
   g) What is important to them beyond work?

2. Prepare a summary of your findings from peer discussions.
3. Set up time to do customer or partner visits with each of your peers.

IV.

The voice of the customer will be channeled through me and market insights will guide our decisions.

DISCOVERING
INSIGHTS

Sales at Domino's Pizza had been in decline for three years when Russell Weiner was brought in as CMO to revitalize the brand and grow revenues. One of the first things on his agenda was to gain actionable consumer insights to inform a new positioning strategy.

"We embarked on a research process to figure out what we knew about our consumer," he says. "What do we know about the pizza consumer, consumers in general, demographics, psychographics, not just people who eat pizza but consumers in general? Then we wanted to know what's going on in the competitive marketplace and the broader marketplace.

"We tapped into a consumer insight that had nothing to do with pizza," Weiner adds. "At the time we were doing the brand positioning, all these banks were going under and folks were asking for bailouts and the bailouts were created by the politicians and funded by the middle class. Consumers were just looking for people to stop lying to them, stop ripping them off and just be truthful and transparent. That was a societal finding, not specifically related to pizza, obviously. But we felt that if we could make it part of our brand strategy, our communication would help us take off because it was something that wasn't just applicable to pizza consumers. It was applicable to everybody."

Weiner is convinced that expansive thinking is critical when determining a brand's positioning. As he explains, "If you think about viewing the ocean from space, it's just this flat mass of water. Every once in a while that water coalesces into a wave, into a big wave. In marketing terms, that wave is a trend, but that big wave is something deep and meaningful that society and consumers are looking for in their lives, with their families, with their politicians. And if you're lucky enough to be a brand whose surfboard, which is your brand positioning, cuts across that wave, you're in a golden place. That's what we tried to do. Would our surfboard be effective in that wave? Could we be the transparent brand consumers were looking for?"

Ultimately, deep market and consumer insights were at the heart of the company's "Oh Yes We Did" campaign in 2010. In the campaign, documentary footage was used to acknowledge consumer dissatisfaction with the core product and reveal — in direct and honest terms — how Domino's was addressing the challenge. Ultimately, the campaign was highly successful and the company finished the year with 10 percent growth.

GATHERING INSIGHTS TO STRENGTHEN YOUR STRATEGY

Successful marketing strategies depend on actionable market insights. These insights provide much-needed perspective on your market opportunities and challenges and help to validate the hypothesis you've developed. By carefully accumulating them you put yourself in a position to make defensible, fact-based decisions as opposed to merely relying on gut and intuition.

However insights, particularly with respect to markets and customers, are valuable in another sense. They reflect the unique perspective and contribution of the marketing department. It is the marketing leader's job to listen to and then articulate the voice of the customer. Marketing is also responsible for recognizing emerging market trends and demands. These are extremely important perspectives that other parts of the organization tend to value highly.

A rigorous commitment to generating insights can produce other forms of value for marketing leaders. Motorola Mobility's CMO Bill Ogle explains how important insights are in terms of developing successful products: "Marketing has to have more than an opinion in product planning discussions. Marketing must come armed with insights about particular market segments as well as the articulated and unarticulated needs of customers."

The ability to draw on these insights strengthens your ability to lead change. You come to the table with facts, not just opinions. This gives you tremendous credibility.

Former Avaya CMO Wes Durow used his analysis of the company's customer database to reveal the tremendously important insight that approximately three-quarters of the company's revenue was being generated from less than five percent of its customers. But the company hadn't been operating with this essential fact in mind. His insight had critical implications for how Avaya should direct its marketing and product development resources.

It's important to think about the gathering of insights in a proactive and systematic way. You'll have to ensure you are collecting the information you need to make smart decisions and formulate a solid strategy and plan. If the information does not already exist you'll need to initiate an insight gathering process to address unanswered questions.

AMD CMO Nigel Dessau told me he created a "fact book" in his first 30 days. This comprised the essential data points he gathered through interviews, reports and analysis of other available research. It gave him a solid set of findings to report to his executive team at the end of his first month. And it strengthened his standing because he presented facts, not opinions.

By embarking on a fact-finding mission in the early days of your tenure you demonstrate that you are serious about identifying the moves that will produce real results. You invite collaboration, openness and honesty. You clarify to your peers, team and wider organization that you are mutually engaged in an effort to discover the growth opportunities that exist for your organization and that you intend to seize them. Rather than dictating a strategy you are engaging others in the process of creating it.

So how do marketing leaders go about gathering necessary insights?

There are a variety of steps and approaches used by the marketing leaders I've spoken with. But one of the most important is simply interviews and discussions. As you interview people both inside and outside the organization you'll need to have a solid set of questions that helps inform the strategy you are attempting to develop.

GE Healthcare CMO Sean Burke likes to ask five questions to everyone he interviews when seeking insights. Whether speaking with fellow executives, people on his team or others outside the organization, he relies on these questions to produce a consistent body of findings.

1. What is our strategy?
2. What are our greatest challenges and opportunities?
3. What is the role of marketing in this organization?
4. How can the marketing team be more effective?
5. If you were me, what would you pay most attention to?

Other ways of gathering insights include primary and secondary market research, customer database profiling and analytical reports from particular executives and managers (examining everything from marketing practices to customer segments to product performance). You may discover insights by examining reports by outside analysts and consultants.

Analytical research of this kind can tell you which marketing efforts are working and which ones aren't, which market segments represent the most growth or profit (and which are unprofitable) and what customer needs or problems are going unaddressed. These insights then form the foundations of your strategic efforts going forward.

One challenge that marketing leaders face is that the insights they are seeking — on markets or customers, typically — frequently don't exist in any form. Customers in the database may not have been profiled. New market segments may not have been identified and analyzed. When gaps such as these exist, it's important to hit the ground running and begin gathering these insights quickly. This is especially true when you are relying on an outside party for independent research.

If you intend to reveal a compelling marketing strategy within your first 100 days you'll need to give your analysts ample time to gather the data you need in order to make informed decisions. There should be a clear sense of urgency associated with this endeavor.

Keep in mind that it may have been your predecessor's failure to gather relevant and actionable insights that has created this opportunity for you. Too often marketing executives are relying on gut instinct to drive their decisions in today's markets. They may not study transactional, behavioral, attitudinal or trend-related data with the care and discipline of a data-driven decision maker.

Don't make this mistake. Rich and relevant data is the thing that will truly make your case powerful and your strategies convincing. This is an element that can set marketing — and *you* — apart.

DISTILLING YOUR FINDINGS THROUGH A SWOT ANALYSIS

The danger you face in gathering all this data and information is that you might drown in it. It's easy to get overwhelmed by the array of possible directions suggested by the facts you put together. With this in mind it's essential to distill these insights into a framework — an overview of your findings — that makes them manageable.

One approach is the "SWOT" model. It's an approach that has stood the test of time and remains popular among the marketing executives interviewed for this book. SWOT, an acronym for "Strengths, Weaknesses, Opportunities and Threats," is a valuable summation tool, providing a clear and simple way to put your key findings together in one place for at-a-glance assessment.

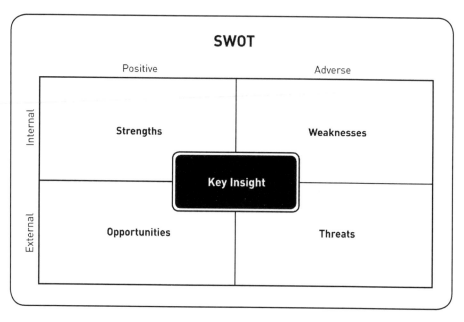

The value of this tool is the alignment discussions that result from your synthesis. By distilling your analysis into short, actionable insights, you can get your executive team on the same page and set the stage for your strategic recommendations that will soon follow.

To help ensure that your findings are most conducive to your alignment conversations, use each quadrant for its intended purpose. Strengths and weaknesses are associated with an internal perspective. These are matters related to what you do well and don't do well. They are shaped within the enterprise and by your current capabilities: What are your organization's strengths and weaknesses? By contrast, opportunities and threats offer an external perspective. They are shaped by patterns and trends occurring outside the organization. They include competitive pressures, market shifts and disruptive innovations: What are the most important opportunities and threats in the marketplace?

Finally, an overriding insight can be derived from your consumer research, your competitive assessment or any other factor outlined in your SWOT analysis. The purpose is to foreshadow the key insights that will drive your strategy. By aligning on these with your team early, you can make sure the energy you devote to developing your strategy will be well focused. There should be no surprises in relation to your recommendations when it comes time to review the strategy with your boss, your peers and your staff.

KEY INSIGHTS TO GATHER

So what are the insights you'll want to collect? Based on my discussions with top marketing executives, the following core set of categories was identified:

- Customers
- Competition
- Capabilities
- Industry trends
- Sales partners
- Culture
- Touch-points
- Measurements

Let's take these categories one by one and discuss how they can contribute to the formulation of a unifying and compelling marketing strategy.

Customers. Marketing becomes indispensable when it keeps a finger on the customer's pulse. It's customer insights that truly elevate and differentiate the marketer's point of view. For the most part other executives and departments have opinions about customer trends, needs and behaviors. But they aren't in a position to capture and analyze the voice of the customer — not in the rigorous and disciplined fashion that marketing can.

Customer insights are derived from a number of elements. One is market segmentation. What market segments are most profitable for the company to address? To answer this question you need a clear understanding of the distinctly different types of buyers for a product, service or solution.

At Anheuser-Busch, Keith Levy segmented the market based on three factors. "We worked with a research group out of Chicago to create what we called our Demand Landscape," he said. "We looked at the beer industry from three different dimensions. The first was palate: What type of products were people interested in in terms of attributes like 'sweet and easy' or 'rich and savory?' Second was in terms of how they used the products — whether it was dining out, at a ballgame or at another type of venue or occasion. And the third dimension was to categorize the type of consumer loyalty. For example: Some people are what we called loyalists and those types of consumers are incredibly brand loyal and will stick with the same brand day in and day out. On the other end of the spectrum are the experimenters: These consumers buy a certain brand today and will likely look to experiment with another tomorrow. They constantly search around to see what's available and what can be newly discovered." The insights from the Demand Landscape helped guide Levy's product positioning and new product development strategies.

At Motorola Mobility Bill Ogle was trying to use customer insights to move the company from developing great products like the RAZR through "random acts of genius" to developing them as a systemized, disciplined and repeatable process. To do this at Motorola variations among smartphone users had to be recognized. What were the differences in how consumers used their smartphones and why did they use them? Instead of trying to create a phone that did everything for everybody (making it too big, too heavy and too costly), the assembly of features was optimized for specific types of users. Such insights enhance product planning.

Consider some of the questions that may be relevant in terms of how the customer is experiencing *your* product or service: How do they find it, buy it and use it? How does it fit into their daily lives? How do you make it easier for customers to do business with you? Customer feedback and other forms of research can help you further enhance the customer experience and begin identifying new products or ways to add value. If this feedback can be systematically accumulated and understood it provides insight into what is working, what's not working and what unmet needs could be better addressed.

Competition. Your ability to provide value to your customers must always be considered in the context of what competitors can offer them. With this in mind it's important to assess your advantages and disadvantages relative to these rivals. How are their brands positioned? What are their products, services and price points? What do their communications programs look like? What customer segments are they pursuing and how are they pursuing them?

By getting fully grounded in your competitors' strategies and approaches you have a firm comparison from which to evaluate your own strategies, plans and actions. Through this lens you can determine what is necessary to differentiate your enterprise and outmaneuver your competitors.

Capabilities. As you are developing your strategy, understanding what your company can actually deliver becomes essential. Denny Marie Post, formerly Chief Innovation Officer at KFC, spent Mother's Day working at a KFC restaurant when she first took her position. It gave her a real sense for the constraints and possibilities associated with developing culinary innovations.

If you want to launch new products or promotions, can the manufacturing or logistics organization execute them? What needs to be changed to make them possible? Do you have the R&D capability to address a particular market need?

Such questions emerge as you begin to explore the market opportunities your enterprise might seize. What you are ultimately challenged to do is find the customer needs that your organization can address profitably and distinctively. By understanding your capabilities in the context of what customers value and the competition can (or cannot) provide, you set the stage for strategic moves that can drive your company to new levels.

Industry trends. You can do anything but you can't do everything. What are you going to focus on? What product segments and market segments are you intent on penetrating? To answer these questions you need to understand your industry and where the growth opportunities lie. What parts of the industry are growing? As Wayne Gretzky famously said, it's about skating to where the puck will be as opposed to where it is right now.

One of the roles of a marketing leader is to help the company understand how trends will play out and what new growth opportunities they will enable. By analyzing industry trends and shifts, you help the enterprise adapt to change and prepare for the fast-approaching future.

Macaroni Grill, for instance, transformed its menu to a Mediterranean style of cuisine as the trend for healthier consumption emerged. The company identified this trend in its research and then embraced it. The objective was to transition from being thought of as simply a pasta-oriented restaurant chain to an eatery that was more aligned with a healthy lifestyle.

Sales partners. If the sales force or channel partners are important to your success, factor them into your research and analysis. What does marketing produce that helps the sales force or how do you go about learning what that could be?

Early on in her tenure as the new CMO for CiCi's Pizza, Nancy Hampton spent time with her franchise partners. This gave her insight into their operational constraints, the consumers they served and the reason they invested to become CiCi's operators. Samsung's Doug Albregts found that gathering insights from channel partners was also valuable. In his role as VP of Sales and Marketing for Samsung's Information Technology Division he asked my firm to elicit feedback from its retail and reseller members. What did they like about the brand, and what were the problems and challenges they were having?

You want to know what you need to do as a marketing organization to drive revenue and enhance sales effectiveness. In many cases your partners are the ones with the direct customer relationships and who carry multiple product lines. This gives them a unique perspective, allowing them to provide crucial input for strategic development.

Culture. Gaining insights about your company's culture is important for many reasons. To lead change credibly you need to understand your company's values and norms, especially if you are coming in from the outside. You want to avoid "organ rejection" syndrome that can occur in companies where forces will be arrayed to protect themselves from you if you don't quickly absorb established cultural norms.

You will often find that culture is also reflected in the company's brand. Take Radio Shack. Under the leadership of Lee Applbaum the marketing team spent a lot of time interviewing employees as part of the brand strategy development process. They took the time to listen to what the frontline people had to say about their company. One thing they heard in the lingo was that Radio Shack employees refer to the company simply as "The Shack" — an insight that helped form the company's brand strategy. In fact a whole campaign and marketing approach was built around insights that came from those employee conversations.

On the other hand it was apparent that Blockbuster was headed for bankruptcy long before it happened. Store service members had become increasingly alienated from the company. When you hear an employee blame "corporate" for procedures that lead to disorganized checkout lines you realize that the employees have begun to check out, too. The fact that they were making these statements with customers standing in line said something about the culture and how it had fallen. The company was ultimately headed in the same direction.

Touch-points. It's essential to ensure that the customer experience is satisfying and consistent. When the customer experience is frustrating or becomes fragmented, your brand erodes. Customers become uncertain about what to expect — or what your brand represents. With this in mind it's necessary to gather insight as to how the organization is performing at various touch-points, such as the call center, the website or the retail store.

Grant Johnson, CMO of Pegasystems put it this way: "I spend a lot of time thinking — and often obsessing — about the customer. We not only need a synchronized view of the customer, we need to synchronize how we serve customers, regardless of the channels they choose — spanning mobile, social, Web, call center or in-store. We have to address customers holistically — to understand and synchronize how customer processes work across our organizational silos in order to improve the customers' experiences and optimize our business outcomes."

Ralph Rogers, the former head of marketing for the Stanford University Graduate School of Business, faced a fragmentation challenge when he tried to align all of the school's departments to provide more consistent and compelling communications. According to Rogers, "There were three degree programs, four research centers, executive education, development, publishing, public relations, alumni relations and many different academic disciplines. Unfortunately, they were each running their own marketing activities with very limited coordination or consistency." To effect change, one action he took was to analyze all interaction points with the outside world and catalogue them. "For the first time, there was a comprehensive review of every way the school was expressing itself externally — whether through e-mails, the website, brochures or advertisements." Once the scope and cost of the communications were documented, it was easier to demonstrate the need for communications alignment and to support the use of a centralized message architecture to help clarify, unify and strengthen the school's brand and messaging.

At GE Healthcare, Sean Burke would bring together a team of salespeople and have them evaluate the marketing team's collateral. Pieces were marked with red, green and yellow stickers based on their usefulness. That was just part of the feedback process, generating insights from the sales organization on what worked from a marketing support perspective.

Measurements. Some of the insights you need may be facts that already exist within the company. What does the company know about what works and what doesn't work? What is currently being measured? Why? What is the data telling you?

You'll want to know if the organization is collecting the right data or just the convenient data. Are the measurement systems set up to help your organization better understand how to make money? The danger is that your organization may be measuring things merely because they are easy to measure, not because they truly matter. It's your challenge at this point to ensure that the measurements you take line up with your objectives.

If you want to grow customer loyalty and profitability you'll want to measure the value of customer segments — and even individual customers. If you are merely measuring the margins on your products you could easily miss the mark in terms of your overriding goals. You'll want to use these measures so your marketing dollars are moving to your most profitable (and promising) customer segments and away from those that are unprofitable and unpromising.

ALIGNING ON INSIGHTS

Marketing leaders typically need about 30 days to address the issues we've raised in the first four chapters. It is during this first month of your tenure that you will learn the expectations of others, introduce your overarching agenda, begin to establish the relationships that will be vital to your performance and, finally, gather the insights you'll need to formulate your strategy.

You'll want to present your key findings and insights to your executive peers and marketing team in order to give them a sense of what you've learned during your fact-finding mission. You'll be setting the stage for the strategy you will be introducing soon. You are revealing your assumptions and the findings that back them up. You are providing a survey of the enterprise, its strengths, weaknesses, opportunities and threats. Indeed, your SWOT summary represents a powerful tool for communicating these findings and inviting further discussion.

Your goal at this point is to align your colleagues with your analysis. By driving consensus around your initial findings and how you've interpreted them you lay the foundations for introducing a new marketing strategy that others in your enterprise will embrace enthusiastically.

ACTION PLAN CHECKLIST

1. Create a list of facts and customer insights you'd like to have before developing your strategy.
2. Identify the facts and insights for which your company currently has data. Review the data and discern relevant facts.
3. Initiate research activities to answer the critical questions for which you do not have data.
4. Set up discussions with at least five customers, five channel or franchise partners and five sales associates or store managers.
5. Prepare your SWOT analysis.

V.

....

*We can do anything, but we can't do everything,
so we must be focused and intentional if we are
to be great.*

....

DETERMINING YOUR STRATEGY

Jim Speros may have been new to Fidelity when he stepped into the role of CMO for the investment firm, but it wasn't his first time to revitalize the brand of a large, complex company. He arrived with a clear idea of what needed to be done having had similar experiences at Ernst & Young and AT&T.

"The primary goal I was asked to accomplish was to pull together a coherent story for the brand. The company had a product-driven brand in the marketplace largely driven by its mutual fund business. There was strong awareness but there was not a cohesive story being told. We needed to pull together all of the communications for Fidelity: advertising, direct marketing, sponsorships, online, social media, mobile marketing, PR. All of the channels.

"At the outset I did some really deep dives into customer insights and research around how customers were feeling, as well understanding how employees felt about the brand. At the same time I began building relationships with other leaders from across the company, making sure I knew where their heads were at and where they wanted to take the business. I also needed to do a deep dive to understand the competitive set, the business and how it made its money so we could push the right levers.

"We had a lot of good work that was already in flight before I got there on defining the company's brand positioning. The core insight was that in the whole financial crisis people had begun to lose confidence in their own abilities and were looking for more help, more guidance on what to do. The fundamental positioning we settled on was that of Fidelity being a guide, navigator and financial partner through the financial journey of one's life.

"But moving from a positioning statement into its expression was where we really needed to invest a lot of time. So we grounded everyone in the positioning and quickly moved to our internal agency as well as our external agency partners. We worked with these teams on an integrated basis and did a lot of ideation and created various campaign alternatives and media ideas. All of it had to be grounded in a core creative idea to be effective.

"When we thought about the creative challenge, a light bulb went off when I was driving home one night and the concept of a GPS came to mind. When you think about what a GPS does, it takes you from point A to point B to point C. It course corrects when you've gone off track. So that became the grounding creative idea for the campaign's expression — that of being your financial GPS through life. We then engaged several creative teams to express the concept in different ways. That work led to the now famous Fidelity 'green line' emerging as the winning creative concept."

Did the strategy work? Looking back on what he and his team had accomplished, Speros concluded that "besides building the employee momentum and excitement around the strategy, which was a big accomplishment, we launched an integrated campaign and saw a 66 percent increase in brand preference. We saw our net promoter scores increase and saw our financials moving positively. When you put all of those points together, it's a pretty good story." As a result of its strategy, campaign execution and results, Fidelity was named marketer of the year by the Financial Communications Society in 2010.

STRATEGY AS YOUR COMPELLING AND UNIFYING IDEA

Strategy can be thought of as *"the* framework by which companies understand what they're doing and want to do, *the* construct through which and around which the rest of their efforts are organized," writes Walter Kiechel, author of *The Lords of Strategy.*

Your challenge as the newly appointed marketing leader is to formulate and execute a compelling marketing strategy. You must decide what your company wants to be from a marketing perspective — and, just as critically, what it intends to do. Your marketing strategy, ultimately, will be nested within your organization's business strategy.

You've been hired to introduce a winning strategy — to take your company in a new direction and outmaneuver your industry rivals. So what makes a winning strategy? What are its elements? What do you need to focus on? How do you go about the process of formulating it?

Rather than focus on specific marketing strategies that you might implement, this chapter will introduce some methodologies for producing your strategy. It will hone in on what matters — and what most requires your attention at this stage.

It's important to be discriminating here. As you know, a company can do anything, it just can't do everything. And so it's critical to select carefully from an array of possibilities and sharpen your focus.

One place to start is with something that can be described as the unifying idea. Some might think of this as the "Brand Purpose," "Brand Promise" or the "Core Value Proposition." It is essentially the idea that unites the whole company, not just the marketing organization, with respect to who you are, what you stand for and how you will win. This becomes an essential element in strategy development.

As the American Marketing Association defines it, marketing is "the activity, set of institutions and processes for creating, communicating, delivering and exchanging offerings that have value for customers, clients, partners and society at large."

As a discipline, marketing is about engaging the marketplace and is connected to everything in your enterprise and, as reflected in your company's brand strategy, marketing is at the heart of the story your company is telling customers. Your marketing strategy will, by necessity, have an influence on (and be influenced by) product strategy, financial strategy and operational strategy. It will also define how you are seen as a leader and will affect the results you are able to achieve. So it's critical to get this right.

THE PAYOFFS OF A MARKETING STRATEGY

Through the process of developing a marketing strategy you can accomplish several objectives that will support your marketing efforts going forward. Most important, you can provide focus, clarity and alignment.

Focus. Your marketing strategy helps to establish where your organization will focus its time, energy and resources. What market segments will it pursue? In which product categories will it invest? How will your company communicate with customers? Your challenge is to answer the question: "What will we focus on so we can win?"

Clarity. This is where you resolve ambiguity and bring greater certainty to the question of how your organization will meet its goals and objectives. You will help set the stage for individuals to engage in activities that will support your larger mission. While you are not yet trying to determine which specific activities are relevant in terms of execution, you are creating an environment in which your people can begin defining those activities for themselves.

Alignment. Your strategy helps various groups and departments — product teams, operational teams, customer-focused teams, etc. — to get on the same page and move in the same direction. You'll never accomplish your objectives if your teams are off on their own tangents, pursuing their own agendas. And the larger the enterprise the more vulnerable it is to fragmentation. Strategy is the vehicle for pulling your organization together.

If a marketing leader fails to develop and articulate a compelling marketing strategy, there will be a lot of wasted energy and people spinning their wheels. The amount of internal angst, frustration and dysfunction will multiply. Moreover, competitiveness will diminish as market rivals capitalize on the company's inability to mobilize and act. Worse, internal groups may even come to view each other as competitors in a struggle for attention and resources. They will try to pull the organization in a direction of their own choosing — filling the vacuum left by the absence of vision and strategy. Everyone will lose sight of the customer — and the real demands of the marketplace. You'll get divergence instead of convergence.

YOUR THREE-YEAR HORIZON

So there's much at stake as you begin to articulate your marketing strategy. You are building credibility and establishing yourself as a leader in your organization. Early on your strategy will be one of the core factors on which you'll be evaluated. It will also be an important test of your ability to align with other executives and engage your organization.

I've found through conversations with dozens of CMOs that it is helpful to think of your strategy over a three-year timeframe. That means the strategy has time to pay off but it's not such a long period that the ideas encompassed within it become abstract. Five-year plans, which might have been popular in a simpler and slower era, are no longer as common. While course corrections and operational refinements will certainly be necessary, your overarching strategy, particularly if it is focused on changing the brand or the business, should have at least a three-year shelf life.

Thinking in three-year cycles not only encourages the organization to think expansively, it reminds everyone that there will come a time when the strategy is up for renewal. At the end of the three-year cycle it may be time for a new strategy — a new beginning. That's fine. Considering the fast-paced nature of today's markets it makes sense to continually refresh a brand's approach or an organization's direction. But not too frequently. If a company is constantly trying to make itself over it will appear lost — and consumers will become confused. By thinking in terms of three-year cycles you create a sense of confidence, commitment and predictability — all factors that are critical to the mobilization of your enterprise.

THE STRATEGIC TRIAD

Your marketing strategy should address three core elements: customers, competitors and capabilities, the "strategic triad." In other words, how are you providing value to your customers? How are you differentiated from your competitors? And how will your capabilities enable you to innovate, operate and fulfill the promises you've made and do so in a profitable way?

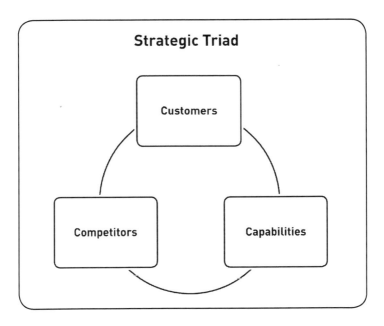

Customers. Everything begins with a customer. Without satisfied and engaged customers you are nowhere. Your challenge is to ensure your strategy addresses the real needs of the marketplace. What customer segments are you targeting? What is relevant or meaningful to your customers (and prospects)? What evidence have you accumulated to make this case? What offers are you prepared to make? Ultimately you want to articulate how you will provide value to customers in different segments.

Competitors. As markets become more saturated and competitive it's no longer enough to provide value. You must provide *differentiated* value. Who are your competitors? What moves are they making? What are their strengths and weaknesses relative to your own? How do you intend to outmaneuver them? How is your value proposition distinct in the marketplace? Can you pursue a strategy that identifies opportunities where there are no direct competitors? By answering these questions you'll show how your company can win within a competitive context. You'll clarify what sets you apart.

Capabilities. You also need to articulate how you will innovate, operate and deliver on your promises. Your capabilities are your essential leverage points — the factors that distinguish you in the marketplace and determine where you will compete. What products or services will be in your portfolio? Which offerings will you emphasize? How will you produce and deliver them? How will your people, processes and systems strengthen your efforts? Perhaps most important, you must show how you are innovating — and intend to continue doing so over time. Whereas innovation was once the responsibility of R&D and product development teams, it is increasingly the responsibility of marketing. Because marketers are the ones listening to the voice of the customer, you have a unique perspective into what the market wants (and will want next).

Your strategy must address all three elements of the triad and the questions they raise. One way of summarizing the essence of your strategy is to develop a positioning statement. A strong positioning statement incorporates the three elements by defining what you do, for whom you do it and what makes you different. This concise statement represents the heart of your strategy. To work as the articulation of your strategy, it must be compelling (to your customers), distinctive (relative to competitors) and true (to your purpose and capabilities).

David Ovens, as CMO of Taco Bell, defined his company's positioning strategy this way: "I'd been with YUM Brands for years in Australia before I took on the CMO role at Taco Bell. I knew that our brand positioning was based on 'value,' but it wasn't clear how value was dimensionalized. If we were going to grow profitably again we needed to be clear on what dimensions of value we were going to deliver. So I laid out three possibilities: price value, abundant value and quality value. I believed we could win on the first two but we had to do things differently if we were going to reclaim our leadership position. After we gained additional consumer insights and studied the dollar menu offerings at other quick-serve restaurants, we developed our new 79 cents/89 cents/99 cents menu. The test marketing of the new menu was a huge success, so we rolled it out nationally later that year."

STAGES OF CUSTOMER ENGAGEMENT

Having a clear positioning is a critical component of your strategy. But it's not enough simply to develop messages for customers. It's also important to prioritize how to connect with them based on their stage of engagement. Is your biggest challenge attracting new customers, converting existing opportunities or reducing churn among existing customers? Maybe you must prioritize between stimulating end-customer demand and incenting channel partners to stock and promote your products. Or you need to be clear about whether building loyalty and repeat visits will have more significant impact on your business than stimulating first-time trial. Remember, you'll want to do everything. But you probably don't have all the resources to do so. You'll have to make choices.

While there are many models for articulating customers' journeys with you, I've found this framework incorporates the best ingredients of many of them. It defines five stages: familiarity, consideration, purchase, loyalty and advocacy. It also recognizes a series of feedback loops and linkages between these stages. By understanding how your brands are performing at each stage of the framework you can align your resources and programs on the stages that will have the most impact.

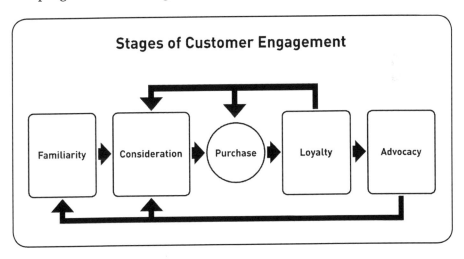

Stages of Customer Engagement

Familiarity → Consideration → Purchase → Loyalty → Advocacy

Familiarity. In the earliest stages of customer engagement the objective is not merely to create awareness of a particular brand or product but to build familiarity. You are trying to create enough interest that your prospective customer will take a closer look at you. Traditional advertising such as television, radio or print can be highly effective in this area. And costly. Increasingly consumers are hearing about new products and services based on what their friends are sharing on social media. This is why the advocacy loop is so important in reaching new customers.

Consideration. Here your intent is encouraging buyers to consider your offering relative to alternatives in the marketplace. Product samples and special offers may play a significant role at this point. Partner relationships can also be particularly crucial, lending credibility to a new or relatively unfamiliar product. Often the first point of consideration is your website or a merchant's site. So making sure consideration assets are well developed and syndicated will be important.

Purchase. The issue at this stage is what is necessary to convert and close. Prospects may go to a retail store with your brand in mind only to walk out with a competitor's product. Some prospects may be abandoning their online shopping carts, raising questions about what must happen in the final stage of a sale to build buyer confidence. Investments in training tele-reps and sales personnel can also be critical at this stage. Or maybe your pricing is not commensurate with the perceived value relative to competitors. Spending lots of resources to stimulate consideration or trial will go to waste if your real problem is a conversion issue.

Loyalty. Once a prospect becomes a customer there can be immense profitability associated with building and strengthening that relationship. The customer's experience must be positive, so assuring customer satisfaction may be an important place to focus your attention. If customer satisfaction is high, investing in customer communications or loyalty programs to encourage cross-selling and up-selling may both strengthen loyalty and enhance profitability.

Advocacy. There's no better source of marketing than a satisfied and vocal fan. With this in mind companies are increasingly investing in social media to identify, engage and encourage their advocates to amplify the voices of their fans. New customers trust other customers more than they trust you, so creating platforms on your website for your advocates to share their ratings and reviews can have a positive outcome on new customer acquisition.

The loops in this framework highlight the connections between loyalty and reconsideration, and advocacy and new purchases. Loyalists are far more likely to consider new products or services from the same supplier but only if they are familiar with the offerings. You can't assume that they know about everything in your portfolio, so crafting an effective cross-selling competency may be necessary if you are sub-optimizing the value of your current customer relationships. Likewise, advocates may be willing to say good things about you but may be waiting for the mechanisms, and encouragement, to do so. Tapping into the power of your fan base will take concerted and consistent effort, so consider incorporating advocate amplification into your strategy.

PREPARING YOUR STRATEGY PRESENTATION

Once you have outlined a strategy you'll want to develop a strategy presentation. Keep in mind, the objective is not to lay out all your tactics in great detail at this point. Rather, you are challenged to get alignment on the high-level direction and the strategic choices you are recommending.

You'll want to articulate your targeting focus and positioning strategy. But you'll want to go deeper. You should explain how you are addressing the various dimensions of marketing: customer segments, products, distribution channels, communications channels and geography.

Finally, you'll want to provide some direction as to how you will engage customers, invest in media and measure your results. You can introduce your framework for tracking and reporting progress.

By providing some overarching direction in these areas you'll give your organization an approach to rally around. You'll provide focus and clarity while helping to establish organizational alignment.

You'll probably deliver your presentation to your boss and your executive peers first — seeking their feedback and alignment. You can then present your strategic view to direct reports and, ultimately, the wider marketing and customer-facing organizations.

AMD's Nigel Dessau offers insight into how he prepared to present his strategy to his leadership team. "There's a period of time when you listen, you put the hypothesis together, you go test the hypothesis, then you put a plan together within 90 days to go execute it," he says. "You know, clearly the first 30 days can't be all listening because challenges are going to come your way, but what I do is begin producing my final presentation almost at the beginning. Then I go through the process of adjusting the hypothesis. The presentation begins with the quantitative data I've learned. Then I'll speak to what I've learned qualitatively. I'll come to a conclusion. Then I say, 'Let me show you where I think we are and where we need to get to.' And then I explain why these are the six projects I'm going to work on. I call them my focus areas."

As Dessau explains, "It's a classic presentation approach: Here's the position, here's why it's a problem, here are the possibilities, here's what I propose to do. In 45 minutes, you want to be able to make that case."

David Roman, CMO for Lenovo, offers another perspective on presenting your strategy for maximum impact: "My charter was to grow the brand. I had three months to deliver the marketing proposal to the executive team on how we were going to do that. I developed a three-component strategy:

1. *Balance*: Between push and pull. Between long-term and short-term. Between lower-funnel and upper-funnel programs. Between 'halo' products and high-volume products.

2. *Simplification*: We had too many sub-brands and designs. We needed a model more like my former company, Apple.

3. *WOW Factor*: We needed to stand out with our products and with our advertising. We needed to choose what was different.

"I then put this framework into the language of the Lenovo Way: Planning, Prioritizing, Performing and Practicing. We said we'd focus on the youth market with unique and compelling products, especially in emerging markets. Once we rolled this out internally, it provided a lot of energy to the company."

Clearly marketing leaders must articulate their strategies to earn the trust of peers and mobilize their teams. As you engage your people in your vision you will be building momentum for change — and confidence that it can be achieved.

PRESENTATION TECHNIQUES

As I've talked with CMOs about how they presented their strategies several techniques were revealed that you may find useful. Among them:

1. **Fact-based problems and solutions**. By highlighting why the status quo must change based on data that others will recognize as true, the need for change and your proposed solutions may be more readily accepted. Example: Consideration rates for the brand have declined. Therefore you'll need to reinvest in marketing programs that build consideration.

2. **Insight and opportunity**. By revealing a compelling consumer insight your proposed approach can be a rallying point for action. Example: Consumers have lost trust in their institutions. Therefore a brand based on authenticity and transparency will resonate in a compelling way.

3. **From:To**. By clearly listing the key elements of the previous marketing approach and your proposed approach you can

provide needed clarity to align the organization. Example: From trying to address all consumer segments shift focus to the youth market.

4. **In:Out.** By specifying which markets, products or activities will receive focus and which ones will not, you can reduce ambiguity in the organization that often leads to conflict and wasted resources. Example: In, smartphones; out, flip phones.

You are now mobilizing for success. The next challenges you confront will concern organizational structure, people and processes. Overcoming these challenges will help you ensure you have the resources and capabilities in place to begin focusing on execution.

ACTION PLAN CHECKLIST

1. Articulate your winning idea in one sentence.
2. List the facts or insights that led you to this conclusion.
3. Outline the core elements of your proposed strategy:

    a) Positioning
    b) Segment focus
    c) Product focus
    d) Channel priorities
    e) Geographic priorities
    f) Customer engagement priorities
    g) Communications investment and mix

4. Develop a *From:To* or *In:Out* list to clarify the changes you propose.
5. List the key allies with whom you should preview your proposal.

VI.

I will lead a high-performance team that will be accountable, agile and aligned.

STRUCTURING
YOUR TEAM

When Kim Feil joined Walgreens as its first CMO, the company was going through a lot of changes. As she explains, "The company was 109 years old. We had 7,600 stores and we did not have a marketing department. What was in place here was a department called Advertising and the Advertising department had three primary responsibilities. The printed circular that goes into the Sunday papers, TV advertising that had no strategy to it and intra-store signage; and that was about it. My charter was basically to install and instigate a highly competent marketing capability to help the company drive growth for the next 100 years. We had an organization that had become very comfortable over 109 years with the Sunday circular being its primary method of communicating and marketing to consumers."

The company was coming to the conclusion that the traditional pharmacy, which had previously focused on filling prescriptions to customers in a convenient locale, was no longer the model of the future. As Feil puts it, "The local pharmacy of the future is really going to be about community healthcare and it is going to expand past pill filling to healthcare services, prevention services, counsel and advice."

Walgreens realized that new positioning and marketing would be necessary. The company also understood it would need to rethink media and channels. It had to go beyond its traditional reliance on the Sunday circular and convenience stores to engage its five million customers in new and compelling ways.

"After doing all my due diligence and working with the rest of the company on what it wanted, I framed out where we had been, where we were and where we were going be," says Feil. "Then I explained that the individuals, their positions and the work that they did was not aligned with what we were going to do going forward. It was more about the organization needing change than about individual people who didn't want to come along. We respected what they had done and appreciated them, but this was how it was going to change."

At the same time that Feil was exploring a new direction for Walgreens' marketing the company had undertaken an initiative called Rewire, which was to look hard at every single department and the way it had been doing business and making decisions. "It was about how to restructure the organization for the new strategy," Feil adds. "What I ended up doing was cutting over half the department. I riffed about 15 people that I did not see coming along and I outsourced 60 for two functions that we were doing in house that made no sense to do in house. We were producing the entire Sunday circular inside the building. Everything. It was ridiculous. There are big companies out there who do it for a living. They run the whole thing now with seven people. We saved $28 million outsourcing it."

STRUCTURING FOR SUCCESS

As the Walgreens example suggests, much of the marketing leader's ability to operate revolves around organizational structure. To put your strategy into effect you'll need the right organizational structure in place. And, to a great degree, your structure depends on your strategy. Your structure will require you to incorporate multiple dimensions of marketing. You'll face questions about what should be centralized and what should be decentralized. And you'll be challenged to determine what should be in-sourced and what should be outsourced.

Questions of structure are critical because they address how you will organize for program execution and how you will handle budgeting to allocate resources. How will you organize teams based on the kind of programs you are going to execute? Will they be product programs, customer segment programs or channel programs? What structure will facilitate the multidisciplinary programs you intend to execute? And how will the dollars for those programs be allocated? What cost centers will be established and who will manage the budgets?

Of course the larger the company or the more diverse its product portfolio the more complex the structure is likely to be. Marketing structure will be affected by the overarching structure of the enterprise, which is why there is such a great diversity among companies.

DIMENSIONS OF THE CMO'S STRATEGIC ROLE

Through my research and experience working with dozens of different companies, I found that there are five dimensions of marketing that ultimately need to be accounted for in your organizational structure. They are: customer segments, products, distribution channels, communications channels and geography. Your challenge is to determine how all five dimensions will work together. Which ones will have primary program management responsibility and budget accountability? Which ones will be supported by the lead team? How will their efforts be integrated and aligned?

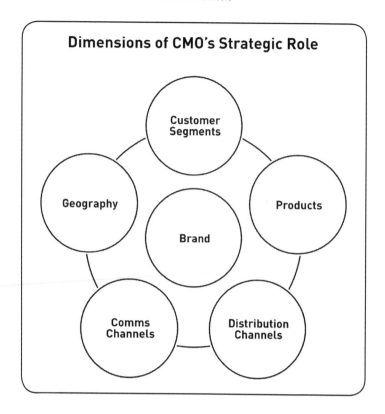

Consider how you will incorporate each of these five dimensions:

Customer Segments. You must determine and articulate which segments you will approach and the specific needs of those segments. The better you articulate this targeting and segmentation, the more your people will be able to develop messages and offers that resonate with buyers. Who in your organization will have the responsibility for planning and managing programs that target distinct market segments?

Products. You'll need to communicate which products you intend to promote and emphasize. You'll need to introduce new product innovations and build compelling offers. You'll also be challenged to optimize your pricing and margin approach — and how it assures competitiveness in the marketplace. Who will manage these activities for you?

Distribution (Sales) Channels. How do you intend to go to market with your offers? How will you support and encourage sales, reseller or franchisee operations? Which channels of distribution will be used? How will you make sure your value proposition is valuable not only to your customers but to your partners? What programs will support these channels? To reach your objectives, your sales engine must be fully operational with well-defined organizational accountability.

Communications Channels. You'll need to express how (and how much) you will invest in various communications channels. What types of programs are you developing and what media will you use to execute these programs? You may be investing heavily in traditional and digital advertising, Sunday circulars, direct mail, co-op marketing, search marketing, social media, loyalty programs or public relations. Whatever your investment portfolio looks like, you'll need an organization to plan, execute and measure these activities. Will you optimize for functional specialization or integrated communications? You'll also need to determine what agency partners will be part of your virtual team.

Geography. The final factor is what geographies you intend to target. Are there specific regions you intend to target for growth and expansion? Is your strategy global in nature? Does your strategy touch on such opportunities? If so, how will your programs be different in various regions or metropolitan areas? How will you drive local market traffic in addition to national brand building? How do you support localized field sales offices? Having an organization capability to manage these issues will be important.

By factoring these dimensions into the design of your organizational structure, you address the questions that will naturally emerge about how your team will support your strategy and the company's diverse marketing needs.

WHAT'S YOUR STRUCTURE?

Through my research I've identified different types of marketing structures that have emerged to balance these dimensions:

- Brand-centric
- Customer-centric
- Channel-centric

Brand-centric structure revolves around individual product brands. Companies in this category are strong in product-based brand management and marketing to relatively homogeneous targets. Procter & Gamble, Dr. Pepper/Snapple Group and other consumer packaged goods companies tend to follow this approach.

Often they have a brand manager who serves as the marketing leader for each brand and is responsible for product innovation, pricing and advertising. In many cases they will have centralized marketing services for functions that bring either cross-brand scale efficiencies, such as media buying, or specialized marketing disciplines, such as social media or market research, to augment the expertise of the brand managers. The brand-centric organization will often sell to consumers through retail channels. Retail merchandising and shopper marketing are often the purview of the sales and retail management group (with a retail marketing support group).

The strength of the brand-centric structure is that it focuses on a brand concept that turns into products to serve specific customer types. Where it is weaker is if there are multiple market segments that are distinctly different. In this case companies tend to have multiple brand managers for multiple brand concepts. You end up managing a house of brands.

The customer-centric structure tends to dominate when companies have direct relationships with their customers as opposed to selling products through indirect channels of distribution. Companies in this category tend to have strong customer relationships and often have challenges managing the brand across multiple market segments.

Dell, for example, emerged as an alternative to retail or indirect distribution, enabling customers to order computers through direct methods. Dell's primary distribution units are structured around consumers, small business, larger enterprise, government and education. (It is further segmented by geography and product.)

In many organizations with customer-centric structures a company has multiple product lines and tries to unify around acquiring and then supporting specific customers. The challenge is keeping a cohesive brand across multiple different customer segments. Another challenge is aligning customer insight and product innovation at a segment level.

Dell ended up structuring some of its products in relation to its customer segments. So instead of just selling servers, desktops, notebooks and services, it is now structured to sell consumer notebooks and business notebooks. It has, in other words, evolved to reflect the customer segment's interest in its business organization.

The channel-centric structure is most common among retailers, e-commerce companies and the hospitality industry (restaurants and hotels). They are particularly proficient at merchandising products. They may be less strong in terms of corporate branding since their programs are often product and offer focused (though there are exceptions). These companies focus on getting the right product line out, priced and promoted effectively. New customer acquisition is less likely to be a metric than transaction volume of specific SKUs.

The restaurant and hotel model tends to be a mix of the brand-centric and channel-centric. The brand leader for a concept has the responsibility for product innovation. Yet much of the marketing features specific items and promotions designed to drive immediate guest visits.

Many retailers and restaurant chains are realizing the value of customer loyalty programs and have built organizational capabilities to manage those programs and associated communications. This is a good example of adapting structures to augment the weaknesses of an organizational bias.

TO CENTRALIZE OR DECENTRALIZE?

If you have a geographically dispersed business or one with multiple business units you'll need to wrestle with the structural question of what should be centralized and what should be decentralized. Determining what marketing functions will be centralized at headquarters and what will happen among the business units or regions is never easy.

Large, multi-line product companies such as General Electric, Dell, Samsung and Dr. Pepper/Snapple Group are particularly challenged by this question. In GE's case the organizational bias is product-based business units. So GE has adopted the model of a centralized corporate CMO who is focused on the GE brand and cross-business-unit best practices, and business unit CMOs who take on the executional marketing responsibility for product-based business units such as energy, healthcare IT and aviation. In Dell's case the business units are customer-based, with a marketing team for each major segment. The corporate function is focused on a unifying brand strategy, the website, social media and corporate social responsibility. Samsung wants a consistent brand across phones and TVs, computers and projectors yet manages its business through regionally based product divisions. Dr. Pepper/Snapple Group has brand managers leading over 100 product brands but has centralized media management and customer insights.

Often the pendulum will swing from centralization to decentralization and back again because each approach has its inherent advantages and disadvantages. The centralized approach offers more consistency, more control and the opportunity for specialization of expertise that is not possible in some decentralized environments. But the decentralized approach can lead to more responsive behavior to business needs and regional differences by giving more responsibility to individual business units. When there is centralization there is more separation between decision bodies and where the action is actually happening. So there are trade-offs between agility and responsiveness on one side and consistency and control on the other.

So what is the overriding principle? Those aspects of the marketing mix that span multiple business units and should have some kind of a common face tend to get centralized. So we are seeing, for instance, more centralized management of websites and social media marketing. There can only be one HP.com, so HP has centralized the responsibility for information architecture and user experience and has delegated content development to its business units.

The other aspect of the centralization-decentralization question is geographic. What is executed centrally and what is executed locally? Again, there is more consistency to be attained through centralization but more agility if execution is local. The problem with many companies is they don't have the critical mass at the local level to decentralize. As a result the emerging model is to conduct a lot of strategic planning, messaging and program development centrally. The headquarters-based organizations craft the program design and then provide the geographically based units the flexibility to execute in the context of their particular regions. They don't have to reinvent the strategic focus. The strategic focus is defined by a centralized group.

THE STRUCTURE FOR A DIGITAL WORLD

Something that is getting a lot of attention from marketing leaders is the question of how they will evolve their structures from a centralized and structured broadcast model to an interactive and dynamic digital model. Grappling with the move from highly controllable, centralized advertising as the primary way of reaching markets to a decentralized and uncontrollable set of dynamics is difficult. This is an era where every customer is a video producer, a publisher, a critic — and customers can, and will, share their opinions with their networks of influence.

Much is riding on how you handle these challenges — do you handle them internally or rely on outside specialists? Whatever you do, you must manage these dynamics effectively to win. To stay on top of changes and demands in the digital realm, marketers are finding they need to operate simultaneously with both centralization and decentralization.

Some elements of digital media are easier to manage than others. Your website is a more mature part of the digital marketing mix. It's also the one place where everything about your company is always available. It's critical to have a coherent user experience — an information architecture designed for multiple types of customers and multiple products. Centralizing the infrastructure and user experience is common, as is putting business units in control of their respective content.

Social media, meanwhile, is exploding in terms of its popularity and complexity. Everything from Facebook to Twitter to LinkedIn is part of the social media mix. You are now challenged to engage your audiences more directly and help facilitate consumer-to-consumer conversations. You need to create a dialogue, not a monologue.

You have to develop ways to amplify the voices of your advocates, giving your fans greater influence. How do you provide them with tools and techniques to make it easy for them to share a favorable opinion? How are you going to resource and organize for this challenge? Who are you going to allow to blog for your organization? Who are you going to allow to comment on other people's blogs? Who can tweet? Who can respond to tweets? Part of meeting this challenge is creating a competency within your organization to address this new way of communicating. For this reason, many companies are choosing to keep social media management centralized until expertise, interaction standards and common practices mature.

As you decentralize social media activities you'll need policies and guidelines explaining how people can act on behalf of your company. But it wouldn't hurt to emphasize three words when providing guidance to employees. Those words? *Use common sense.*

TO IN-SOURCE OR TO OUTSOURCE?

So what's the role of your internal organization and what's the role of your virtual organization of external partners? It's clear you have options. You can rely on advertising agencies, interactive firms, market research firms and call center service providers to produce marketing services without actually having to develop them internally.

What should stay inside the organization and what can be delegated to an outside specialist?

Frequently the role of the outside firm is to bring a new level of expertise that is difficult to build internally. Advertising firms bring creative talent that is hard to hire (and keep) internally. Some of these activities will always be better left to outside specialists. In the case of Walgreens, the printing and production systems were optimized outside. Or take a website development project. You may not want to staff internally for the peak of a big project like that. It may make more sense to hire an outside firm that can manage projects that involve a great deal of short-term staffing and specialized skills.

By contrast other activities can eventually be brought inside. If you are trying to roll out new approaches and you aren't sure what will ultimately become standard operating procedures you can use outside specialists that excel at those disciplines while you figure out what is going to work the best. Over time you can operationalize these activities and bring them inside. One example is social media work. There are people who understand how to do that very well and if you are just dipping your toe into the world of social media you may initially want to rely on an outside specialist. As progress is made and the work demands become clearer you can begin to hire people internally to take on the role on a day-to-day basis.

One area where questions of in-sourcing versus outsourcing get interesting is in the contact center. Many companies have come to the conclusion that they can reduce costs by outsourcing customer service and other forms of customer contact — often sending these activities offshore. What they may have missed is that these customer interactions represent an opportunity to build customer value — even up-sell and cross-sell complementary products. Whether you ultimately decide to keep these activities in-house or rely on specialists, it's become apparent to a growing number of marketing leaders that such forms of customer contact are not something to be treated in an unserious manner.

Dell, which took a serious public relations hit in the mid-2000s when it outsourced customer service activities abroad, has since brought many of those activities back in-house and, in many cases, back onshore. The company was not about to outsource if it meant undermining the customer experience — a core factor in its brand reputation.

RESTRUCTURING FOR CHANGE

As a new marketing leader you are expected to drive and lead change. Your decisions about structure will have an essential impact on your change efforts. They will also influence your personnel decisions.

By smartly structuring and restructuring your marketing organization you'll be in a stronger position to execute the strategy that you've begun to formulate. You'll have an organizational design that matches your imperatives and objectives. Take advantage of your first 100-day window of opportunity to make the changes your organization needs. It is one of the most visible and enduring decisions you will make.

ACTION PLAN CHECKLIST

1. List the critical marketing functions your organization needs in order to be successful.
2. Structure the organizational "boxes" you would ideally like to have.
3. What functions do you need to add? Eliminate?
4. How will you handle each of the five dimensions?

    a) Customer segments
    b) Products
    c) Channels of distribution
    d) Channels of communications
    e) Geographies

5. Which activities will be centralized? Which ones will be decentralized to business units and regions?

VII.

My team can expect its teammates to be capable, committed and collaborative and the roster will change until those expectations are met.

LEADING
PEOPLE

When Denny Marie Post started her new role as CMO at T-Mobile she knew she had to establish her credibility quickly. Having been a seasoned marketing leader at KFC, Burger King and Starbucks, the telecommunications industry was new to her. So realistically what did she hope to accomplish in her first 100 days?

"I really was hoping to be in a position to accelerate my climb up the learning curve," she says. "I was also hoping to complete an immersion course on wireless. As I look back on it, knowing the industry was far less critical in many ways because there was a safety net around me. I was hoping to have the really important relationships resolved and then my primary goal was to make sure I had my team structured right. I made a lot of shifts in structure in those first 90 days. I restructured the function. And then I dealt with a few folks who other people had passed along. I feel that's often a relief to the team that someone is willing to take action on people everyone acknowledges are probably ready to move on."

Post promoted individuals within the organization. "The organization had a history and a belief structure that you never made it above director," she explains. "The organization would always go out and hire for a VP and above. So I found two young but very capable directors that I was able to bring up to the VP level. I kind of stretched and gave them a shot. I also went out and recruited some talent. In this case, the hires were acknowledged experts in their field. So I was able to do that as well."

THE POWER OF YOUR PEOPLE

As Post's story suggests, your ability to perform will be determined largely by who you lead and how you lead them. Your approach to building a team, managing your people and encouraging employee engagement is central to your success as a marketing leader.

People are at the heart of a high-performance marketing team. But who are the key people that you are going to build your team around? Who are the top performers? Who are the underperformers? In whom can you place your trust and confidence?

Your first 100 days represent a critical period in terms of getting the team right. In my research I found that one of the most common regrets of marketing leaders is failing to act more decisively and swiftly with regard to building the team. Too often individuals are allowed to linger in roles for which they are ill-suited — or they are kept on the team to avoid the conflict of letting them go. Inaction of this sort can lead to painful consequences over time, undermining the momentum of the team overall.

Smart marketing leaders take advantage of their first 100 days to assess and evaluate their people. They look to them to articulate their strengths and weaknesses as well as the strengths, weaknesses, opportunities and threats of the organization. Such conversations can be extremely revealing. They can help you uncover what an individual participant has to offer — and whether the person may prove more of a problem creator than a problem solver.

Bill Ogle of Motorola Mobility sought first to understand, then to be understood. "I asked each of my direct reports to recommend changes we should make to improve the business," he says. "How they responded was very insightful and helped me assess the roles they were going to play on my team."

It may seem disruptive and painful to fire people in the earliest days of your tenure. Many people who've been given new positions naturally resist it. But your leverage to create a high-performing team will never be greater. This is an opportunity to collaborate with your counterpart in human resources to figure out how to make difficult people decisions — and make the right ones. There's already an expectation that a new team will be built. It's best to meet this expectation by creating a team that gives you full confidence.

CHARACTERISTICS OF AN EFFECTIVE MARKETER

Ideally everyone on your team would be a top performer. But what are the characteristics that make a member of the marketing team effective? Sean Burke, CMO of GE Healthcare IT, shared the profile he uses that was developed under the leadership of GE's CMO, Beth Comstock.

"A good marketer has four 'I's," he explains. "The first 'I' is an instigator, the next one is an innovator, the next one an integrator, how you leverage and integrate across all the functions. We started with those three and then one of the business leaders said, 'That is great but you have to add implementer.' I think the great marketing leaders, whether as individuals or as members of a team, are able to perform all those roles. There are examples of great marketers who have come in strong and have played the instigator role. They told their team why certain team members were wrong, they introduced changes they wanted to make, but they couldn't pull everybody together to mobilize that change, then they failed after a short time."

After you have learned your company's culture and defined your strategy, you should have a clear idea of the characteristics that will be important for your people to possess. In my firm, I look for people who typify the phrase "excellence without arrogance." Starbucks looks for people who smile. Brinker International looks for "the hospitability gene." What are the characteristics you will be looking for?

WHO SHOULD BE ON YOUR TEAM?

When JP Morgan merged with BancOne, Eileen Zicchino had to quickly assess the potential effectiveness of people to determine who would remain on the consolidated team. What traits did she look for? "Technical competencies aside, we needed people who would be willing to do what it takes as quickly as it takes to make the change," she says. "We knew that this would be difficult so we didn't need people who would be very high maintenance themselves in terms of needing constant reassurance. We needed the people who had the leadership skills to drive something forward and wouldn't make excuses for making things happen. For example, we knew that we had overlap and that we would have to reduce head count, so when we talked to people about making those changes we asked, 'Can you do this and how would you do this? How would you feel about doing this?' What if this is the person you have known for 10 years? We had to pick people who would do the right thing for the company and would do so in a compassionate way. I think we were pretty lucky there."

To better evaluate your team members it helps to understand the contributions they have to offer — and to accept the possibility that some may be undermining morale. With this in mind, and based on dozens of conversations with marketing leaders, I've identified five categories in which team members can be categorized.

While efforts to categorize people are inevitably imperfect you are nevertheless challenged to make some important people decisions in a short period of time. You may have more success making these tough decisions if you have some kind of framework to help you make them.

In considering how your people might be categorized you can draw on multiple inputs. You'll rely on your own personal experiences, as well as meetings and interviews with team members. You'll rely on personal reputations — both within the marketing organization and beyond it. You'll seek advice from people within the marketing organization and outside it. You also will want to rely on your advisors in the human resources organization. They may have their own set of strategies and frameworks to support you.

This framework puts people in five categories: stars, hard workers, misfits, undesirables and wild cards.

You'll want to consider how these categories lay out on a matrix of current impact and potential. Current impact considers the level of performance individuals already bring to the marketing organization, while potential takes into account their capacity for further growth and development.

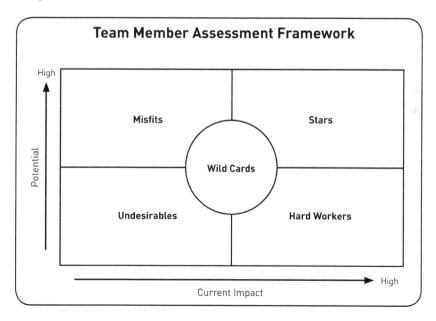

Stars. These are people who are exceptionally gifted. They have the talent and the drive to be valuable leaders. They don't necessarily have to be your direct reports. But as you recognize their leadership qualities you'll want to promote them. In doing so you demonstrate to the organization what behaviors you recognize and reward, whether that be a promotion in terms of job title and responsibility, an increase in compensation, support through advocacy or all of the above.

Your stars are high contributors and have impressive potential as future leaders and performers. You want to lock in your stars and make sure that they feel they are part of, and want to stay part of, your team. Remember, your stars are probably the ones who have the highest number of options outside the company. You'll have to handle them with care if you want to strengthen their loyalty and avoid losing them.

Hard Workers. These are your most reliable and dependable workers. You can always count on them to deliver. As the designation suggests, they will work hard to get the results that are expected of them. While the hard workers may not have all the talents or capabilities of some of the stars, they can nevertheless be counted on to produce. You can place your trust in them and know it's well placed.

Your hard workers are high contributors but don't necessarily have a great deal of room for growth. Your role with hard workers, generally speaking, is to encourage them, support them and recognize and reward the value they are delivering to the team. You want to ensure that their work is meaningful — and they believe it to be so. Loyal and engaged workers are the backbone of your operation.

Misfits. These are individuals who may have much to offer but aren't delivering to expectations at this point. It may be that they are in the wrong roles — or perhaps their direct supervisors are doing a poor job of developing them. With the right actions you might be able to turn them into high performers.

Your misfits are delivering a low current contribution but represent high potential — or at least it appears so. Given that they may be in the wrong roles, your challenge is to try to reassign them to something that is a better fit for their potential, where they will become assets for the organization.

Undesirables. These are individuals who are undermining morale and performance within your organization. They tend to be disengaged and their poisonous attitude can lead to the disengagement of others. They may be angry. They may be dissatisfied. But you shouldn't be focused on trying to placate them. They are deadweight.

Your undesirables are both low contributors and have low potential. Your challenge is to identify these individuals and let them go. You have no choice. People like this can have a terrible impact on your organization, undercutting everything you are trying to build.

Wild Cards. These individuals are the ones who are hard to read. They may seem to be low performers but, in fact, they may have much to offer. They may be burned out or have been underappreciated by previous management for their efforts yet they may have the potential to be strong contributors if managed well. Or there may be individuals who were gunning for your job but lost out to you. These persons would obviously have desirable skills and qualifications, but can they overcome the disappointment and actively support you?

Your wild cards lie in the middle of the chart. You're uncertain where they are or where they will end up. But you sense that they are worth some risks. You want to give these people more time, energy and effort. You want to find out what they are capable of delivering. Given a chance they may prove to be some of your most impressive stars.

As you survey your circle of talent you have to be as rigorous and as clear-eyed as possible. It's easy to misinterpret, misdiagnose or assess incorrectly. People who appear to be extremely supportive may be acting in counter-productive ways behind your back. At the same time people who appear to be difficult employees may be some of your most loyal, committed and even promising ones.

Still others may be extremely influential. They may have political connections they have built over time in other parts of the organization. They may be a favorite of the sales leader or the top engineer. They may appear to be pulling their weight but, at the end the day, they may not be performing in your favor. Alternatively they may be getting their jobs done but simultaneously destroying your ability to form a high-performance organization. These are some of the obstacles (often cleverly hidden) that might stand in your way as you begin building your team.

Ultimately some of your greatest successes may come from identifying misfits and wild cards. These are people you can turn into high performers — hard workers, even stars. They may be suffering from fatigue. They may have lost their belief or confidence due to missteps that had been made in the organization prior to your arrival. They may simply be waiting for you to prove yourself as a leader so they can take confidence in following you. By reinvigorating the team (and, perhaps, by taking a special interest in them) you may be able to bring these people to new levels.

FIVE DIMENSIONS OF EMPLOYEE ENGAGEMENT

Today's business leaders face a myriad of challenges in what continues to be an unpredictable and complicated business environment. It is your job to grow the business, maximize profits, acquire new customers and retain your existing ones. You are also ultimately responsible for creating an inspiring culture, leading change initiatives and keeping your employees engaged.

Successful companies understand employee engagement is a powerful strategy for driving organizational improvement and business results. Research from Gallup and Towers Watson shows companies with highly engaged employees typically outperform their competitors in earnings per share (EPS), growth rate and other financial results.

Unfortunately, recent surveys have reported that only a small number of employees are truly engaged in their jobs. One recent survey from Opinion Research Corporation found that 80 percent of respondents would consider leaving their employers if presented with a new opportunity and 25 percent are planning to leave once the job market improves. These figures are not surprising given the actions many companies had to take in order to weather the economic downturn, which included hiring freezes, pay cuts and layoffs.

Through research done at my agency we have come to believe employees view engagement across five core dimensions. Your organization needs to focus on fostering these dimensions year-round to achieve optimal results.

Belonging. Engaged employees feel a strong connection to the company on multiple levels. They identify with the company's core values and understand how their individual jobs support the overarching mission. If your company's mission and values are not explicitly defined, this is a great project to initiate. If they are defined, find tangible ways to incorporate them into company culture, processes and systems so they are constantly reinforced on a daily basis.

Inspiration. At the end of the day employees want to feel a sense of purpose and know that their efforts matter. Employees have to take pride in what the company does and trust their leaders. Outline a compelling vision for the future, communicate it with passion, acknowledge any challenges or setbacks, ask employees for suggestions and involve them in driving positive change.

Understanding. Clear and timely communication is one of the most important drivers of employee engagement. Your employees need to have a solid understanding of company goals and the specific plan to achieve them. Leaders should provide frequent and transparent business updates and create an environment in which employees feel comfortable asking questions and providing input. At the individual level employees should receive meaningful feedback on their performance at regular intervals throughout the year. Use these opportunities to provide affirmation to your strong contributors and have candid discussions with employees who are falling short of expectations.

Support. Employees feel supported when they have strong relationships with their managers, positive interactions with colleagues and access to the resources they need. Leaders should evaluate both hard and soft skill sets when filling management positions, and they should provide training to help new managers succeed in their roles. Look for ways to provide systematic support for your employees in the form of eliminating unnecessary red tape, simplifying work processes and creating a culture of open communication and collaboration. Tools like the DISC assessment and Myers-Briggs personality test can help to achieve the desired culture of openness.

Appreciation. Employees need to know that their contributions are noticed and appreciated. The significance of sincere praise from direct managers and senior leaders is often underestimated but can be extremely meaningful to employees. Compensation is important and should be competitive, but many employees often rank other factors like career development and learning opportunities above pay in job satisfaction surveys. Get to know your individual employees and understand what each values. Then look for ways to show your appreciation in those specific areas.

How effectively is your organization delivering across the five dimensions of employee engagement? If you have not yet put mechanisms in place to measure and monitor engagement levels, take charge now by asking your employees for their candid feedback. Anonymous engagement surveys can provide visibility to help companies prioritize and focus their efforts on the areas that will resonate most with employees. A successful engagement strategy will take time and effort, but the benefits to your organization and bottom line will be well worth it.

GETTING TO KNOW YOUR PEOPLE

Ultimately your ability to build and lead a team will depend on your ability to engage your people. Your challenge is to build trust and confidence while inspiring belief in the changes you are ushering in.

If you reach out to people and make yourself accessible you have a greater opportunity of winning hearts and minds. Denny Marie Post's Day One activities at T-Mobile included meeting her team:

"The weeks before I arrived in the office, I sought out and met one-on-one each of the individuals who would be reporting to me. The first day I was in I went and spent time with each of them, wandering their part of the department. I had about 200 people on my team in total. So the first day, and for the first several days, I made it a point to walk to see the people in their office environment. The CMO's office, along with all the other executives' offices, per the CEO's demand, was on the 10th floor. The marketing functions were down on the second and third floors. I went to their space, which was something that apparently had not been happening. I got them to walk me around and introduce me personally to the people on their team. I was very much focused on meeting the individuals and taking a measure of the team and their attitudes. It is amazing that the smallest thing can make a difference. To this day they still say they remember that moment, when the new marketing leader actually walked into their cubicle sat down and had a brief conversation, made observations and made some kind of connection. These are individuals who felt that nobody in the company knew their names."

In your efforts to listen and learn, bring some rigor to the process. While exit interviews are common in corporate America, try holding "engagement interviews." Instead of merely learning from employees when they are walking out the door, learn from them while they are still in their roles. You can put together a set of questions — maybe even conduct in-person interviews. You want to know: Do your people believe they are being effectively managed? Do they believe they are being appropriately recognized and rewarded? Do they understand how the organization's strategy connects to their work? Are they proud to tell people where they work? Such questions can provide valuable insights that help you lead at a new level.

But it's not just listening that builds engagement. It's also support and feedback. While you won't be giving all your people feedback and valuable assessments you can certainly do this with your direct reports. You can model the behavior you'd like them to apply with their own reports. Feedback is the means by which you let people know that you value their work and intend to hold them accountable for fulfilling their promises. You provide perspective and guidance, enabling your people to learn, improve and, as necessary, course correct. You want to give them challenges that stretch their talents and enable them to grow — though not challenges that are beyond their capabilities.

Finally you want to create an environment that encourages active participation and collaboration. The tone you set with your people at the outset is particularly important. Peter Horst of Capital One Bank established four operating principles for his organization: clear accountability, brilliant execution, bold moves and seamless collaboration. He insisted on "no drama, no intrigue and no in-fighting," which is not easy to achieve. It starts at the top by declaring a zero-tolerance policy and then reinforcing it with actions on a daily basis. Yet in the end it creates an environment that is not only more fun to work in but one that is more conducive to high performance.

The more engaged your people are the more successful you are likely to be. Your challenge is to identify the factors that might be undermining engagement and eliminate them while amplifying the factors that will enhance engagement. You can begin by evaluating your team members more thoroughly. As you discover the people who can bring the most value to your organization you'll determine how best to invest your time in talent management.

ACTION PLAN CHECKLIST

1. Set up one-to-one meetings with staff members to explore their interests, aptitudes and attitudes.
2. Secure feedback from key internal constituencies about your team members.
3. List 3 – 5 criteria that you and your direct reports will use to assess the talent within your organization.
4. Identify at least one star (assuming you have one) and promote her/him.
5. Identify at least one misfit or undesirable (assuming you have one) and reassign her/him or let her/him go.
6. Present your new organization chart with people assigned to their roles.

VIII.

We will find the right balance between chaos and stifling bureaucracy so that we can do remarkable things as efficiently as our business demands.

DEFINING PROCESSES

Charlie Young joined Zimmer Holdings with a strong appreciation for the benefits of operationalizing the marketing function. After integrating dozens of acquisitions at GE Medical Systems and divesting several companies at Tyco, Young knew how to make an immediate impact as the new marketing leader of the global medical devices company.

"Coming into my role at Zimmer there was a strong belief that we needed to be much more flexible and much more responsive to our customers," he says. "We especially needed to help our field organization be more effective in front of the customer. So I began helping to architect how we could put some of those programs in place, and it evolved into an initiative that we called 'Customers First.' It was the beginning of a broad platform of tactical and strategic actions to create the most customer-focused culture within our industry.

"Under different circumstances that exact approach might not have been my first priority. But I clearly saw this perceived 'gap' as a huge opportunity for the marketing team to build credibility by taking the lead on an important initiative that helped the entire company by sinking our teeth into what Customers First really meant. We drove this initiative very hard — especially as a catalyst to reinforce across the organization that marketing was going to be responsive to the leadership team, to be adaptable and to be accountable for driving results."

While there was consensus on the strategic direction, Young realized he would need to be specific with his tactics in order to operationalize his strategy across the company. "We framed it in a manner that engaged all employees to look inside their organizations and identify areas where we could be more responsive to our customers," he explains. "We needed to look at what we could do to be less bureaucratic and more agile in our internal operations in order to better serve customers. That subsequently turned into hundreds, if not thousands, of great ideas that bubbled up from all over the organization.

"Zimmer had launched similar initiatives in the past but we did not have the staying power to drive deep and lasting change. In this instance, we learned from the past and hired a dedicated Customers First leader whose full-time job is to further accelerate and operationalize our customer responsiveness efforts."

TURNING PROCESS INTO PREDICTABILITY

Enduring growth cannot be achieved without a commitment to process. In the absence of clear processes and methods for how to get things done, companies act in an ad hoc and inconsistent fashion. Indeed, they rely on individual heroics — something that can't be reliably repeated or sustained.

As a change agent in your organization, you to define how you will do things differently and repeatedly through process. You are codifying your new approaches so that your people can act. In fact, your vision and strategy are unlikely to be realized unless you can change the way things are done. Process translates your new direction into meaningful and actionable activities. In Young's case at Zimmer, that meant translating "Customers First" into specific operational processes across the company.

You will be unable to accomplish your larger objectives if you can't produce results consistently. When the organization is a black box of undefined activities, it is difficult to predict how it will perform. It will be unclear how it might respond to the changes you are promoting. Will departments work together or remain siloed? Will important insights and critical information be shared? Will key actions be synchronized? Will all elements needed for success be in place?

An apt definition for process is: *a structured and integrated set of activities that are performed to achieve a defined business outcome.*

You need not become bureaucratic but you should embrace process discipline to bring order, repeatability and predictability to your activities. As you execute processes again and again you can refine and enhance them. Don't get bogged down trying to be perfect. At this stage speed and clarity are more critical.

YOUR CORE MARKETING PROCESSES

Since every organization is different, you'll need to determine the core processes that you and your team will need to function effectively. To help you kick-start your process planning here is a list of core marketing processes that have proved most important to the success of marketing leaders I have interviewed.

Resource Allocation. Getting people and funds allocated to implement your marketing strategy will be critical to your success. Too often, money and other resources are allocated based on past behavior or through ad hoc means. In order to effect change you will need to direct resources to the most impactful areas, which can sometimes mean dramatic shifts from the status quo, as it did for Kim Feil at Walgreens.

To ensure you are managing resource allocation as effectively as possible, you'll need to have a defined budgeting process. Typically, the marketing budget will both reflect and influence the larger budgeting process for the enterprise. The more diligently the marketing budget process is managed, the more credible your efforts will prove to the CEO, CFO and other executive team members who can influence or determine the size of your overall budget.

Your portfolio allocation of those resources is the next issue. My business partner and former worldwide marketing leader for Dell, Tom Martin, put it this way. "Just as a personal financial advisor's results are determined by how they allocate your investments across stocks, bonds, cash, real estate and other asset classes, your marketing results will be impacted by where you choose to deploy your resources." What process will you use to make these decisions? Zero-based budget requests by department? Funding requirements for strategic initiatives? Modeling based on ROI of past programs?

Finally, how will you determine budget accountability? Who are the budget "owners?" Brand managers? Marcom managers? Regional marketing managers? Channel managers? How you structure the rows and columns of your budgets has a huge impact on how programs will be planned and implemented. Do you want to bias action by functional disciplines, by market segments or by products/brands?

Market Segment and Product Planning. The chicken-and-egg problem that every marketing leader must face lies in products and markets. The question is: Do you start by defining the markets you wish to penetrate or do you start by clarifying the products you intend to promote?

If you start with markets you may be unsure at the outset what exactly you are offering. You will be attempting to grasp what unmet needs customers are experiencing within a somewhat vaguely defined area. If you start with products you are committing to develop first and hope that you're going to hit a target that remains to be determined.

One way or another you'll need a process. Market segment planning requires market analysis. How are segments defined in meaningful ways for your business? How big are the addressable markets? What are the gaps in consumers' experience? What might they be willing to pay for a certain, envisioned offer? Do you need to focus on customer acquisition, existing customer growth or customer retention and loyalty? How have the individuals or organizations you are targeting dealt with certain issues to this point? By addressing these questions in a rigorous fashion, you gain a clearer picture of your market. You are gathering input and insights that can strengthen product development and go-to-market programs.

Product planning also requires a commitment to research and development. You'll capture the voice of the customer. You'll assess the merits of new technologies, test new flavors or decipher new financial regulations. You'll define appropriate features and capabilities. You'll develop brand names. And you'll set the stage for your rollout.

Of course it's possible to pursue both approaches simultaneously, but most companies have primary planning biases. Synchronizing the two approaches will often produce the best outcomes. Market segmentation analysis will provide signals to guide product developers. Proposed products will provide hypotheses to test for customer acquisition or market development programs.

Bill Ogle as CMO of Motorola Mobility was looking for ways to turn product development from "random acts of genius" into a more defined and repeatable process. He accomplished this by embedding customer insight and market research far more deeply in the product development process. Through greater integration of product planning and market segmentation planning the organization was able to accelerate product development cycles and more closely match the demands of a fast-moving market. He admits he "hadn't fully overcome the chicken-and-egg problem, but had learned to make a tasty omelet."

Engagement Planning and Execution. Ultimately your plans must be executed in a real-world context. You must engage your customers. You must address questions such as what customer touch-points or communications channels you will use and how you will coordinate your brand and message across them. You'll have to examine paid media (e.g., broadcast advertising and paid search), owned media (e.g., website and direct mail) and earned media (e.g., press coverage and social media sharing) to determine how to engage your customers most effectively.

But how will all this get done efficiently and produce the desired results? Who determines the targeting and messaging for specific campaigns? Who determines the unifying idea and then how does that cascade down into specific communications channels? How will you enforce message consistency across channels? How will you determine the products and offers to be featured? Who briefs the agencies? Who approves the media plan? What decisions do you want to be involved in and which ones will you delegate? These are all questions that you will need to answer.

When action planning is discussed later in the book I'll present some frameworks that may help you and your team answer some of these questions. For now think about the cross-department nature of planning and executing engagement programs. Providing clear expectations of how you would like to see the team operate will reduce organizational friction that could inhibit the speed of your progress.

Customer Acquisition and Lead Management. What is the process that you'll use to acquire customers? This process may differ significantly if you are reaching out to businesses as opposed to consumers — though the more precise differentiator is often whether your customer is engaged in a considered purchase versus an impulse buy. Whatever the case you have to give significant consideration to the question of how you will attract prospects and convert them into customers.

Too often companies stumble at various stages of this process. It may be that marketing and sales are not aligned and, therefore, the sales group is not performing effectively. It might be that consumers are abandoning their online shopping carts and not completing the purchasing process. Browsers may not be turned into buyers because retail staff is inadequately trained. Every company needs to understand the process by which prospects are turned into customers. By identifying the breakdowns in this process organizations can enhance their conversion rates and revenue numbers.

Quite often the biggest stumbling block is getting all relevant parties to understand all the stages of the process. Do they understand what drives buyer familiarity, consideration, purchase, loyalty and advocacy? How does a buyer move through this cycle? How is a lead managed and assessed? When key members of your marketing and channel organizations understand the stages of the customer engagement process with greater insight they are in a position to take action and enhance outcomes.

As prospects become customers new questions come into play. You want to know what must happen to ensure customer satisfaction and success. What will make them loyal, engaged customers? What will encourage them to act as advocates on your behalf and encourage other prospects to become customers? By diligently managing the customer engagement process you can determine how to amplify the value of your existing relationships. Take some time to map out the most important touch-points and organizational responsibilities. If there is confusion try to bring some clarity so your goal of growing customers is not inhibited for internal reasons. Grant Johnson of Pegasystems talked about the importance of synchronizing the organization to deliver great customer experiences. What is your process for achieving synchronization?

Promotion Planning. The process of planning promotions can be quite complex. Special offers, for instance, can take many different forms. Will you offer "buy one, get one free?" How about 79 cent, 89 cent, 99 cent value meals? You may also have co-marketing promotions, sweepstakes or in-store sampling.

What is the process for determining when to run a promotion, what promotions to run, which channels to use for the promotions and the the overall objectives of the promotions? The logistics systems required to implement promotions — whether coupon redemption, free offers for additional merchandise, fulfillment of that merchandise offer, contest compliance processes, etc. — can be demanding.

As you know, there are many sub-processes related to the macro process of promotion planning. The key is to get a handle on these issues and be confident your organization has all stakeholders (marketing, sales, legal, operations, IT, etc.) working collaboratively with appropriate checks and balances but in a way that doesn't grind ideation and implementation to a halt.

Local Market Activation. One of the challenges companies now face is taking their national brand programs and applying them at a local level to attract customers. This concept applies to global companies that are intent on reaching buyers in different countries as well as companies that are attempting to apply national programs to various regions within a single country. Either way the company has a set of centralized assets and resources and now must determine how best to tailor them to the geographically concentrated audience that is being targeted.

Does your company need to align national campaigns with the local market activities of dealers or franchisees? Such efforts are certain to go more smoothly if a defined process is laid out. The process might concern funding activities — such as marketing development funds — or campaign assets that can be tailored to local market needs.

In direct sales organizations the focus often is on field marketing. What discretion does the local team have in creating new programs and materials? How are they supported from the central office? What approvals and reports are expected?

So what is your process for activating local market campaigns? How do you create standards or guidelines so you don't have to pre-approve everything? How do you fund local organizations or franchisees and provide them with materials and other relevant support tools? How do resellers understand your co-op program and get reimbursed in a timely manner?

Website Management. Your website is the one place where everything in the company comes together across products, across markets, across all of your initiatives. Given its reach and potential impact, the site raises a number of process questions.

What are the processes for gathering business requirements and for planning the information architecture for the site? How will it be maintained? Who is responsible for the user experience design and new functionality? How are data and security concerns managed? How is content produced and managed?

If you are a national restaurant chain, for example, with hundreds of locations, how do you localize content for your website? Do you reflect distinctions and changes in hours, menu and promotions? If you are a global marketer, are you going to have elements of your content versioned for different languages? How will your site reflect different promotions and consumer interests in different regions, countries and cultures?

Chris Curtin, Senior VP for Marketing Strategy and Innovation at HP, found that a centralized/decentralized framework worked best for his multi-business-unit, multi-national enterprise. Technical considerations and user experience design were managed centrally. Content was designated as a business unit responsibility and translation verification as a country-level role. HP.com is a huge site — 14 million words are added each month. So during a recent site redesign, all 300,000 employees operated as the quality control team. A special button on the site, visible only to employees, allowed them to notify the Web team of any bugs or errors.

Who will lead your Web initiatives? How will the IT organization be involved? How will you reflect the brand strategy appropriately? Will you develop a mobile version of the site? How will content be syndicated to channel partners? These are the tough process questions that often delay much needed improvements to this critical resource for engaging customers and partners.

Social Media Management. Social media is a rapidly evolving force that raises a host of questions. How are you monitoring social media conversations? How are you participating? Who can participate on behalf of your brand? Who can write blog posts? How do you produce and syndicate shareable content? Who is encouraging your advocates to share their opinions?

Social networks such as Facebook, LinkedIn and Twitter have obviously created an array of new opportunities for engaging customers and prospects. Other sites such as YouTube, FourSquare and Google+ further contribute to the opportunities for outreach. Ratings and review sites such as Yelp and Trip Advisor enable consumers to offer their own evaluations of brands. Given the existence of such sites it's increasingly important to monitor and react to reviews in support of your brand's reputation.

As social media becomes an active part of the marketing mix it's important to define the processes associated with it. This will enable your people to embrace and turn social media into a vehicle for deepening customer connections to your brand.

Naturally there are concerns about how social media is used. Several brands have been harmed by employees who engaged in embarrassing behavior online. This is where standards and policies can be useful in ensuring employee actions are appropriate. Some industries, such as banking and pharmaceuticals, have evolving regulations that must be considered.

The bigger question is how companies can influence the perception of their brands or even attract customers in this exploding social media space. Chili's, for instance, has identified over 400,000 brand advocates: individuals who have high net promoter scores and are willing to recommend the restaurant to others. Through the Facebook Like button brands have an opportunity to encourage such recommendations — and even contribute to their contagiousness.

TIME FOR PROCESS DISCIPLINE

Process is critical to executing your winning strategy. You'll need to emphasize process discipline to bring order, repeatability and predictability to your organization.

Your first step in imposing process discipline is prioritization. Which processes have the most impact on your business success? Once you have identified your most important processes you can take action to begin refining and enhancing them. You'll want to make them as clear, definable and as trackable as possible.

Your next step is to assign (or acknowledge existing) process owners for each of the key processes. Who will have primary responsibility? Will you entrust particular individuals or will responsibility be shared across a group (or groups)? You need to have process owners who can report on progress and problems — people you can hold accountable and celebrate for their successes.

In assigning (or acknowledging) these roles you'll need an approach for process management. One simple approach that my agency uses and often recommends is called RACI. That's an acronym for "responsible, accountable, consulted and informed." The purpose of this framework is to ensure completion of tasks and deliverables in a formal process.

Responsible. Those who do the work to achieve the task. There is typically one person with a participation role of *Responsible*, although others can be delegated to assist in the work required. This could be a brand manager, a channel marketing manager or any member of your team.

Accountable. The person ultimately accountable for the correct and thorough completion of the deliverable or task, and the one to whom *Responsible* is accountable. In other words, an *Accountable* must sign off (approve) on work that *Responsible* provides. It's best to have only one *Accountable* specified for each task or deliverable. Frequently, this person is you.

Consulted. Those whose opinions and insights are sought and with whom there is two-way communication. Also referred to as Contributors since these parties contribute to the planning and execution of your programs. They are often members of other parts of your organization, such as Finance, Operations or Product Development.

Informed. Those who are kept up to date on progress, often only on completion of the task or deliverable, and with whom there is primarily a one-way communication. These are individuals or groups who will be affected by your activities, such as sales, retail centers or marketing functions peripheral to the core decisions.

This framework will help you keep track of what needs to be done — and who is responsible for getting it done. By bringing greater discipline to the challenge of process management you help your marketing organization produce results predictably.

ACTION PLAN CHECKLIST

1. List five key processes that will be most critical to your immediate success.
2. For each process describe the desired outputs of the process and why the process needs to be improved or made more clear.
3. For each process, identify the involved parties and designate them with one of the four roles:

    a) Responsible
    b) Accountable
    c) Consulted
    d) Informed

IX.

*Our plan of action will have an emphasis
on action.*

PREPARING
YOUR PLAN

Mark Addicks is no newcomer to his role as CMO at General Mills. He's been a marketer at the company for over 20 years and has served as CMO since 2004. He oversees hundreds of brands, from Cheerios to Yoplait Yogurt, and mentors a myriad of new marketing leaders every year. Yet he has never been complacent when it comes to learning and implementing new marketing planning techniques.

"We constantly look for other companies big and small that are outperforming the market. We go out and speak to them and start to discern what are the best practices. One of the best practices we found was building a marketing plan that is simple, action oriented and succinctly states what the elements of the marketing plan are going to be. We saw that in small firms and we saw that in big firms. We borrowed and learned from other people and developed a one-page document we call our Plan to Win.

"It starts with succinctly stating the one business challenge that's standing in the way of growth and the specific metric, such as market share percentage, you want to grow. And then we ask based on that challenge: What is the business insight about that challenge that your brand could uniquely answer or own related to that challenge?

"Therefore what's going to be your 'idea to grow?' Then from your 'idea to grow' we break that down into five elements that we want to be addressed succinctly:

1. What is the campaign that you're going to launch that's going to get people to act now?
2. What kind of product or innovations are you going to put into the brand experience to support that campaign?
3. What are the margin enhancements you're going to champion so that you're adding more value to that experience against that challenge and cutting off the things that have less value?
4. What unique things are you going to do at a retail level to bring this to life?
5. Price and value. What is going to allow you to optimize price or value for the consumer?"

As you can see from Addicks' framework, it is in the planning stage that you are challenged to translate your marketing strategy into executable activities. This is where you make your strategy for change tangible and actionable.

FROM PLANNING TO PAYOFFS

It's worthwhile to step back and think about the larger picture here. Your high-level marketing strategy, which is nested within your enterprise's larger business strategy, is comprised of several dimensions. These dimensions, as we've discussed in chapter 5, cover brand, customer segments, products, communications channels, distribution channels and geography.

But now you are challenged to create an overarching marketing plan, which will make your larger strategy more concrete. To do so you'll need to create a set of *action plans* that cover all aspects of the marketing mix. These action plans, which may have different owners with dedicated responsibilities, will roll up into your overall marketing plan. This plan, then, becomes the playbook for future action.

While your strategy focuses on setting direction and making strategic choices, your plan lays out the actions that will enable you to pursue your strategy and meet your objectives. This will enable you most effectively to allocate your resources, conduct activities and hold your team accountable for results. The plan will serve as a framework for getting things done.

The overarching marketing plan is the tool for ensuring your various action plans remain consistent and aligned. Your advertising plan, for instance, should be connected with your product plan and your channel plan. Your marketing plan is one vehicle for addressing the danger of organizational silos and miscommunication.

Your marketing plan is also a vehicle for budgeting. If your strategy is focused on global growth, for instance, you'll want to budget appropriately to deal with regional issues. If your strategy requires you to target new customers you'll want to budget appropriately to reach these new segments.

The default action plans that you inherited may no longer work. You may have to change your regional plan because of growth opportunities in the developing world. You may need to change you communications plan because Sunday circular advertising isn't providing nearly the lift that it did in past years. As with many other companies you may be shifting an increasing portion of your budget to digital marketing and social media activities. You may need to rethink segmentation. Indeed, it may be time to reconsider the mix of investments devoted to customer acquisition relative to customer retention and advocacy. It may be more profitable to grow revenue from existing customers than find new ones, despite the request from sales for more leads.

Your planning process is going to bring many issues to the fore. The question is how planning effectively will help you address them.

INTUITIVE AND ANALYTICAL PLANNING

One distinction that emerges among marketing leaders lies in their general approach to planning. The two types of approaches that I've witnessed are the intuitive and the analytical.

Intuitive leaders tend to plan with great deference to what seems to have worked in the past — or what seems most likely to work in the present. There's a tremendous reliance on experience and instinct. The leader might adopt plans that have worked in other organizations at other times. Or that leader may gravitate to particular positions because they seem appropriate to the moment. Marketing leaders who specialize in brand transformation or advertising-driven marketing might be especially likely to adopt this approach. This leader may be drawn to the "big idea" and focus on spreading that idea throughout the organization. The intuitive approach is common where there is urgency for fast action and a dearth of reliable data. Steve Cullen, SVP of SMB Marketing for Symantec put it this way, "A good plan executed today is better than a great plan executed later."

Analytical leaders, by contrast, rely heavily on data and rigorously generated insight. Their plans can be thought of as models. They are looking for data or input to feed into these models — and they are looking for outcomes to guide their next set of moves. They will actively rely on scorecards, dashboards and reporting from the field to make their decisions. Their plans will reflect this sensibility. They will be deeply interested in efforts that involve testing, learning, measurement and refinement. Many of these types of leaders have emerged in transaction-oriented businesses where direct marketing or e-commerce has played a prominent role in growth.

Of course marketing leaders are rarely exclusively one or the other. These distinctions merely indicate a tendency. Intuitive leaders are likely to have well-honed instincts. Analytical leaders will rely on their data-driven experiences. But what is their predominant approach when it comes to planning? What is yours? If you know your leanings, you may be well served to seek out a lieutenant who can offer some balance and contrast. After all, Kirk (the intuitive) relied on Spock (the analytical) to run the Starship Enterprise. It makes sense to seek out someone whose strengths complement yours.

Whatever your approach you are going to have blind spots. It's critical to recognize the inevitability of this dynamic and seek ways to address it. While the intuitive leader may need assistance in generating more data to guide and defend decisions, the analytical leader may need assistance in communicating ideas to the organization and inspiring commitment. The planning process represents an excellent time to address these blind spots so your marketing strategy is articulated clearly and executed effectively.

INTEGRATED MARKETING PLANNING APPROACH

As you begin to lay out your plan, consider a series of steps that will help keep your team aligned and engaged. Here is an approach we use at our firm to help ensure our clients are addressing strategic planning challenges and laying the groundwork for effective execution.

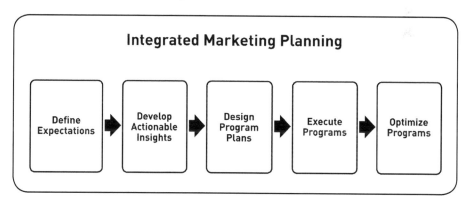

First you want to *define expectations*. You want to make sure you are pursuing the appropriate objectives and have aligned your efforts with the overall business and marketing strategy. Here are a set of action steps to consider:

- Confirm overarching corporate goals and business initiatives
- Define supporting marketing initiatives with clear objectives and supporting strategies
- Identify key constituents to be targeted within the initiatives
- Align on sales, product and operations organizational requirements
- Allocate associated budgets for each initiative

Second you'll need to *develop actionable insights*. Here is where you get a firm handle on your marketplace, competitive landscape and customer dynamics. Much of this may have been gathered in preparation for your strategy development. Now it's time to get even more specific and tactical.

Here are some action steps to consider:

- Review competitive analyses to define the opportunities most specific for you; this could include identifying an underserved segment or a competitor whose customer base is vulnerable
- Gather customer insights, including path to purchase analysis, media consumption and psychographic segments most aligned with your value proposition
- Conduct research, if needed, to gather a more accurate view of current perceptions of your brand, attitudes about your proposed offerings and opportunities for engaging buyers in unique ways
- Develop personas of your most important buyers so that all of your departments are working from a clear and consistent view of the desired targets

Third you *design your plan* for marketing programs. Here you clarify and formulate the specific programs that you plan to implement. Action steps to consider:

- Develop clear and succinct value proposition statements and highlight any innovations to be developed
- Articulate the positioning and key messages for each program
- Develop audience maps for each program
- Define sales channel and/or sales force issues that must be addressed
- Develop demand-generation frameworks for each program and target (more on this methodology later in this chapter)
- Define required integration points across the organization
- Determine content that must be developed for each program
- Allocate budgets to specific tactics
- Enroll regional stakeholders for alignment and adaptation

Once you have outlined your overall plan and spelled out the specific programs you wish to implement you'll want to review some key documents that your team will use as it prepares to *execute programs*. Here, you define the actual tactics necessary to achieve your objectives. Consider reviewing:

- Specific measurable objectives for each program
- Campaign briefs used to direct your agencies
- Creative concepts developed by your agency partners or internal creative teams
- Regional adaptations of the program plans and creative (if needed)
- Project team members and key project milestones, including major cross-department alignment points
- Measurement and review plans for all programs (prior to program initiation)

Finally you need to plan now for how you will *optimize your programs* after they are launched. You will be relying on feedback and reporting to assess and refine your approach. The time to clarify how you will be involved in assessing program progress and making ongoing optimization decisions is at the front end, not at the post-mortem. Action steps to consider:

- Agree to program dashboard elements
- Outline the reporting and review process
- Define parameters for optimizing programs that require your involvement

While this model is meant to be illustrative as opposed to prescriptive, it shows how you can lay out your marketing action plan into a set of coherent steps — making it clear to all participants what actions must be taken to produce tangible results.

VISUALIZING YOUR PLAN

One reason you have documented plans is to ensure all teams members know what needs to be done and their roles in the process. One way you can help improve understanding and align support for your plans is by showing the flow between activities. We've devised a tool called the Customer Engagement Framework, which shows the interactions of your activities from the customer's perspective.

This approach provides important benefits. First it creates a visual expression of all the elements of the plan and how they are connected. If someone is managing a website or a call center, for example, that person can understand where he or she fits in the process.

Second it allows you to define precise measures for specific activities within the workflow. For this example you can measure the number of leads you intend to produce and vividly show how you intend to produce them.

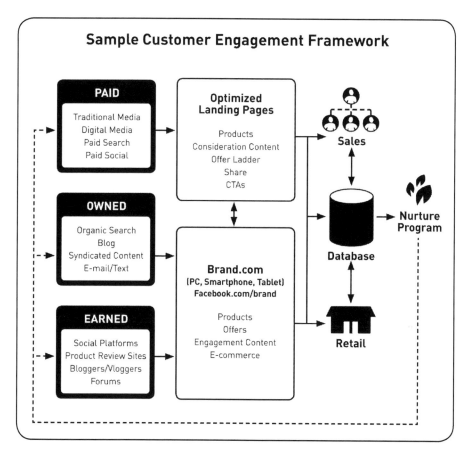

The third (and probably the most valuable) benefit I've seen produced from this approach is highlighting gaps in the process. For instance I have seen situations where marketing attracts prospects to a website and encourages them to register, but there isn't a database set up to capture the data or a call center to handle the follow-up of leads. By highlighting gaps you can determine what actions are necessary to manage a lead, engage a customer or complete a transaction. And, by making it visual, you make it far easier to identify and discuss these gaps.

This visual approach adds a clarifying dimension to your plan. It illustrates what you are going to do and how you are going to it. But it also helps your team members better understand how the plan works. Some say a picture is worth a thousand words. But sometimes it's worth more. If the picture enables you to clarify a complex process and achieve alignment around a sophisticated plan then it may have accomplished more than a thousand words ever could.

PLANS VS. PLANNING

You build credibility for your action plans — and thereby your overall marketing plan — by clearly stating what actions you will take, explaining the logic behind them and by demonstrating how you are going to execute them. By identifying what gaps may exist and then showing how you will close them you make your plan even more defensible.

Your planning process may involve multiple lieutenants reporting to you, the marketing leader. Their jobs may be to own and carry responsibility for individual action plans. For example, you may have a product marketing director who manages the pricing plan, a marcom director accountable for the communications plan, a channel marketing manager who owns the channel plan and regional marketing directors who manage the geographic-focused plans. No matter your structure your team leaders' roles are to produce and manage the action plans that will roll up into your unified marketing plan.

What's important to understand is that much of the value of the plan itself is the discipline of planning. The facts on the ground will continuously change. New findings in the field will require course corrections and program refinements. The plan itself should be dynamic — subject to continual refinements. But having a rigorous approach to planning that encompasses your biggest marketing concerns will always pay handsome dividends.

The discussions in the conference rooms, or even heated debates in your office, that help the formation of the plan will be important. Enrolling your team in developing the detailed plan helps build their accountability for the results and their understanding of the interdependencies. Do not rush through these discussions. Sure, you want to avoid endless debates that never lead to decisions. But good candid conversations among your team leaders during the planning process can yield future benefits for you and them.

And remember: You don't need large, complex, overly detailed plans. While the "thud factor" associated with dropping such a plan on a desk may seem impressive, such weighty tomes are only likely to create confusion and misalignment. When developing your plans it's much better to focus on clarity and alignment. You want to do what it takes to produce results.

ACTION PLAN CHECKLIST

1. Define the key initiatives or programs that you plan to implement.
2. Adopt a framework or series of frameworks that your team can use to develop plans to support these initiatives.
3. Outline the steps and timetable for your team to develop supporting plans.
4. Establish a cross-functional review process so your team leaders can share their plans with their peers.
5. Establish clear accountabilities for who is responsible for which action plans. Use the RACI method to provide specificity in roles.

X.

We will embrace feedback, stay attuned to market dynamics, learn what works and optimize accordingly.

MEASURING
PROGRESS

When Martyn Etherington arrived at Tektronix in 2002 he inherited an organization with marketers spread across multiple functions and multiple geographies. "I looked at all of the objectives from all of the product lines and we had somewhere above 100 strategic objectives, 4,000 activities and were unable to measure anything other than dollars spent; and we weren't very good at that either. There were no success criteria.

"For our 'Get Well Plan,' we distilled the objectives down to 10, simplified our charter, defined the success criteria, centralized the organization and the accountabilities, aligned ourselves to shared goals and put compensation plans in place for my people in the regions tied to their sales peers, so immediately they had skin in the game. And then we started to focus on the organization alignment around metrics. Measurement and accountability became a mantra. We didn't necessarily know at that time what we were going to be measuring but really declared the focus from Day One.

"And then probably the best hire I've ever made was putting a marketing operations manager in place. He was the combination of a Rottweiler and a Golden Labrador. That was the type of person I needed to help me implement a planning process and a monthly reporting process. We started with 'measure what you can' and built from there. The concepts of ownership and accountability were probably equal or more important than the results early on. What we looked at were three primary measurements. Effectiveness: What are we doing to move the needle top line bottom line? Productivity: Were we adding value? And efficiency: Were we doing things efficiently?"

When asked what in his background led him to this kind of analytics-based approach to doing business Etherington turned to a movie reference. "It was probably less about the data more about performance. I'm not sure if you saw the movie *Money Ball*. Billy Beane wasn't necessarily interested in the data — it's about the performance. How did he actually optimize the performance of his team? And that for me was more interesting than the actual data. It was about performance and continuous improvement.

"I focused first on efficiency and then moved to effectiveness — my primary goal was growth. Like Billy Beane, I needed an operations manager, who was an absolute fanatic on numbers, to complement my vision and passion for performance with his for numbers and analytics."

THE MEASURE OF A MARKETER

Now that you've unveiled your strategy and have presented your plan, expectations are high. Your board, your executive team and others throughout your enterprise are all looking for signals that you can produce compelling results. The language that will resonate most with them is the language of numbers; effective measurements will be critical to meet expectations. It's the means by which you will mark your progress, demonstrate performance gains and build confidence that you can meet your commitments.

As I think about the subject of new marketing leaders and metrics I am reminded of a meeting in spring 2007 where I was presenting the findings of a quarterly marketing measurement review to Jeff Barney, the newly appointed head of marketing for Toshiba's U.S. notebook business. My firm had been working with Toshiba for several years in planning, executing and measuring advertising and e-commerce programs. Over several quarters we had refined a quarterly business review comprised of measures that included brand consideration, Web traffic, ad interaction rates and program efficiency trends. Prior to Barney's appointment as the marketing leader he had been the head of the division's business planning and finance organization. As a result he had an intimate understanding of the multi-billion-dollar business unit's P&L.

During the long meeting, Barney asked lots of simple, yet insightful questions, among them:

- "Why is this measurement important?"
- "What is the data telling us we should do differently?"
- "How did we establish that goal and is it still the right one?"
- "How does that measure connect with our revenue or unit plan?"
- "Where does that data come from?"
- "What should we be measuring that we're not measuring now?"

The way he approached marketing metrics was analytical and directly connected to the business performance for which he was accountable. Having previously been the budget approver, he now was responsible for ensuring that the division's marketing effort delivered results. The questions he asked are the questions all marketing leaders should ask.

Through core measures and key performance indicators you'll reveal marketing's impact on the enterprise's top and bottom lines.

You'll show your return on marketing investment — and build the case for further funding your top initiatives.

In a recent study by Columbia University, *Marketing Metrics in the Era of Big Data,* 70 percent of marketing execs reported that their marketing efforts are under greater scrutiny than ever. Yet fewer than half were making budget decisions based on ROI data. Two-thirds were making decisions based on historical activity and instinct. Is it any wonder why CMOs are struggling to gain credibility in the C-suite?

But it's not simply a matter of accountability. Measurement is the means by which you can optimize your performance, refine how you allocate resources and adjust your plan based on what programs are and are not working.

WHY MEASUREMENT MATTERS

Measurements are a way of aligning the expectations of the marketing team across your business. Kim Feil of Walgreens put it this way, "I explained to my peers the framework that I was going to use for approaching marketing and the discipline I was going to use, including the measurement system, because that is what keeps the integrity in the decisions I was going to make. I was not going to make a lot of progress by trying to explain how I work with an ad agency to create positioning and getting the approval to make that decision. I just made it. The way I kept it transparent was by putting marketing score cards in place, putting metrics in place to show whether we were making good decisions or not. Exposing our output instead of exposing what decision rights I was going to take. 'I made this decision. Here is why, here are the facts to support it, and if you have any input, I will take it, but we are moving forward, right?'"

Measurements are also a tool set for keeping your people focused on the right things. Doug Albregts, whose marketing leadership positions include vice president of sales and marketing for Samsung's Enterprise Business Division and president of Sharp Imaging and Information Company of America, put it this way: "The best business advice I ever got was simple but quite impactful: 'If you can't measure it, you can't manage it.' By having defined measures my team knows what they are accountable for and it gives us non-subjective feedback on whether we're making progress."

CHALLENGES TO SUCCESSFUL MARKETING MEASUREMENT

When taking a new role as a marketing leader, one of your immediate challenges will be to identify the metrics that matter to your enterprise. Some measurements and reporting processes may be in place. But you'll also have an opportunity to introduce new performance indicators and find new ways of collecting missing data.

Let's explore some of the problems with implementing a better system of measurements that you may encounter when you assume your new role:

- Existing metrics may be insufficient or inappropriate; as a result your organization may be optimizing its efforts around the wrong measures, which will lead to poor business decisions
- Your marketing team may lack the capabilities, competencies or skills to gather or analyze the metrics you need
- You may not have adequate tools or processes for capturing, analyzing and reporting on you findings – and making forecasts in relation to them

Consider these one by one.

First, you may have a problem if existing measures are insufficient or inappropriate. There is an old joke that you've probably heard that illustrates this issue.

A man who has obviously had too much to drink is bending over under a street light looking for something near a parked car. A passerby notices him, then stops and asks, "Are you looking for something?"

The drunken man replies, "Yes, I dropped my car keys and I can't find them. Would you mind helping me?" To which the passerby replies, "Happy to help. Is this where you dropped them?" "No, my car is down that way a few yards in the dark." The befuddled passerby then asks, "So why are you looking for them here?" The drunken man calmly replies, "Because the light is better down here."

While this may sound silly, I've encountered this at several companies with which I've consulted. One was an information services company that optimized its marketing efforts around two key measures: number of leads and cost per lead. While this doesn't sound problematic on the surface these measures led to programs optimized to generating a high volume of low-cost leads. As a result the firm was attracting small companies that frequently switched suppliers, which led to a high-churn, low-margin customer base. The company's stated desired was to penetrate high-margin, high-lifetime value segments, yet its efforts had been misdirected based on the measurement system.

Issues similar to this may have been one of the reasons your new company sought you out. If the prior marketing leader was unable to connect the marketing activities and the business goals through a measurement framework that made sense to other executive leaders it could have diminished their trust in your predecessor. If you have strong ideas on the matter you may well have a relatively free hand implementing them. But before you do you'll want to test your ideas out on your executive colleagues and build consensus around them.

On the other hand you may perceive inadequacies in the existing measurement and reporting systems that others don't recognize. You may, in fact, have clear ideas about new measures you'd like to introduce. While you may run into some resistance when making these changes, your outreach to other executives — such as the CEO and CFO — gives you an opportunity to gain their buy-in with respect to these new measures and how they are reported. Your discussions on the matter can even enrich your understanding of marketing measures as they will be perceived by others in your organization — and what they value the most.

The second potential challenge is related to the capabilities and competencies of your marketing staff. Does your team have the skills and resources necessary to gather, analyze and interpret the data you need — and produce the findings you seek? If not, you may have some new hiring decisions to consider. You'll want to bring in people, such as Etherington's marketing operations manager, who are capable of handling the measurement challenges you face. It's possible to consider training and developing your existing team members, though you may want to treat this separately as you have some urgent issues to address in your first 100 days. For the time being you may have to go outside the organization and bring in an advisor who can help you manage the immediate challenge of establishing a measurement framework and setting up systems that work.

Keith Levy faced a variation of this problem when Anheuser-Busch was acquired by InBev, a company known for its tight financial operating practices. "Anheuser-Busch in its heyday was very much a right brain culture of ideation. The new culture was more of a legacy InBev mindset, which was much more of a scientific, left brain, process-oriented marketing approach. And so we had to evolve to a new way of evaluating things through a more uniformed dataset. As a global company, A-B/InBev was trying to find synergy in our approaches to analytics and innovation that could be transferred across zones around the globe. So we were moving toward a uniform dataset and sometimes we ran into problems. A-B had this rich history of data, and as we began using a new dataset we really didn't have the history right. So we were trying to make decisions on limited information. But that was a temporary issue. As time went on the data got more complete, more robust and there weren't as many issues."

Which brings us to the third challenge associated with measurement. Do you have the tools and processes in place to meet your measurement objectives? As with many companies you may find that relevant data is trapped in silos throughout the enterprise. Identifying where this data resides and what it takes to gather it may be your first issue on this front. You'll need to determine what tools and infrastructure will be necessary to gather and interpret this data on a regular basis. And while there is much talk these days about creating automated dashboards that provide real-time insight into activities and outcomes, such concerns must follow considerations about creating the right measures, gathering the right data and interpreting it in the right way.

BUILDING YOUR MARKETING MEASUREMENT SYSTEM

As you begin to formulate your approach to marketing measurement you'll need to address these issues and challenges with your own solutions. You'll want to seek out the advice and guidance of those you trust — and those you most need to trust you. You'll want to lean on the best practices and insights available for your core measurement issues. What measurements are most appropriate? How will you build measurement competence and a culture of performance? What tools, processes and systems need to be in place to engage in successful measurement? These are the questions that you'll be challenged to address at some point in your first 100 days.

What measurements are most appropriate? While there is extensive debate on such matters and what you choose to measure will largely be situational, there are some patterns that seem consistent across enterprises. Through my discussions with CMOs it appears that marketing metrics tend to fall into one of four general categories: brand metrics, sales metrics, customer metrics and marketing efficiency metrics.

Brand metrics are assigned to the reputation your enterprise is building or depleting in the marketplace. Measures include how your company or product brands are perceived by customers and prospects as well as other stakeholders such as employees, partners, regulators and industry influencers. They include longer-term components such as awareness, familiarity, consideration and preference as well as shorter-term components such as social media conversations, buzz scores and media coverage.

Sales metrics provide you an indication of your impact on your ultimate goal: generating revenue. Internal reporting is normally the source of most sales data. But to assess performance relative to competitors, many marketers turn to sales data from third-party research firms. The frequency of the reporting can vary from weekly to annually, making these sources more or less useful in optimizing your activities. Because there are many factors involved in generating revenue, correlating marketing activities to sales results is a common challenge. How sophisticated you want to be in building the correlations will depend on your business and your organizational capabilities.

Customer metrics are linked to the value of your existing customer base. You want to know the size and the lifetime value of existing customer relationships. With this knowledge, you can determine which customer segments represent the most profit and which ones the least. You can make assessments of current share of wallet and potential growth opportunities. Some of the smallest customer segments may have tremendous potential and, vice versa, some of your most profitable segments may represent little opportunity for further growth. Some customers may be "net promoters" while others are "net detractors." These are the kinds of strategic metrics you can compile to target the right customer segments and take action to deploy programs with the right focus.

Still other metrics are concerned with the efficiency of your marketing programs. You can measure the return on investment of campaigns and programs to determine the impact of marketing investment decisions. You may even rely on media-mix models to determine the appropriate mix of media placements, messaging approaches and offers that will prove most profitable. Such measures can help you optimize your allocation of resources while strengthening near-term results. Wes

Durow found that a systematic approach to measuring the efficiency of his marketing programs worked well for him when he was CMO of Fonality, a company that sells cloud-based telephone services to small businesses. "By working with our agency we were able to improve the ROI of our lead-generation programs by 4X in six months."

While the challenge of synthesizing these metrics to create a comprehensive view is a significant one for most companies, it's clear that you have much to gain by producing metrics that address all four of these dimensions: brand, sales, customer and marketing efficiency. By ensuring you are tracking all of these dimensions at a high level you gain a stronger grip on the essential issues that will influence your performance in both the short and long terms.

How do I build measurement competence and a culture of performance? To meet these objectives you'll need to attract and retain individuals who bring the unique skills you need. You'll need to emphasize and reinforce measurement. Some top managers require their people to develop a business case in order to get funding approved for any significant project — and then they hold them accountable for meeting the objectives to which they have committed. Indeed, it's likely that your CFO will require that of you. When you have a performance culture decisions rest on data, facts and figures. You demand evidence and analysis to justify action — and to communicate results.

You can contrast this approach with a culture of intuition. Such cultures are driven primarily by experience. While there's nothing wrong with experience it's not enough in an unpredictable and fast-changing environment. Experience can't tell you what programs or campaigns will work. It can't tell you which customers are the most profitable or the most promising. Such insights require measurement and analysis. They require a new skill set that has not been common in the marketing organizations of the past. However, it's increasingly common today. Marketing leaders at companies as varied as Amazon, Harrah's and Capital One now rely on analytical work to drive decisions and actions.

Many large organizations are finding value in establishing marketing operations departments. Their primary functions are to help manage the resource allocation and budgeting process for the CMO across all business units, marketing disciplines and geographies and to establish measurement and reporting frameworks for all funded initiatives. By centralizing this expertise you can have the capability to audit program effectiveness within your organization and a hub for sharing key learnings across your organization.

What tools, processes and systems need to be in place to engage in successful measurement? One of the most unifying activities that marketing leaders can initiate is to develop a marketing dashboard. Dashboards represent a reporting tool that provides you a comprehensive view of major activities, trends and points of progress (or regress). You can capture what has happened retrospectively and what is likely to happen prospectively. That said, it's important to recognize that these tools need not be automated. Whatever the dashboard ultimately looks like or how quickly (or slowly) data can be pulled into it, the point is to have a window on your marketing efforts — an ability to report on your performance.

This presumes you have access to the data you need to build relevant and reliable reports. The adoption of analytical tools — enabling predictive and retrospective analysis — has played an important role in enabling marketers to identify customer segments that are likely to be receptive to particular offers. Campaign management tools enable marketers to manage and track their campaigns intelligently. Another class of tools enables marketers to track interactions at various touchpoints such as a website, in the contact center or, increasingly, through social media. And still other tools enable marketers to integrate and manage customer data.

This growing portfolio of tools is an important factor in your ability to gain insights into marketing and customer interaction activities and, thus, measure performance with greater speed and precision. These tools, in turn, will help you respond more quickly to market trends and predict emerging trends with greater success.

But it's not always necessary to acquire and integrate new tools, technologies and systems. And you don't have to go it alone. In order to accelerate your learning and adoption of new capabilities you may consider bringing in consultants or selectively outsourcing activities to marketing specialists. However you get there it's clear that the clock is ticking. The more rapidly you can get effective measurement capabilities in place the more quickly you can produce the results you've committed to deliver.

CAPITALIZING ON YOUR MEASURES

Measurement is often discussed within the frame of accountability. It is seen by others as a means of holding you accountable. Perhaps you see it as a means of holding others accountable. That's fine as far as it goes. Everyone should be more accountable and act more responsibly. Everyone should work diligently to meet goals and keep commitments.

But that's not really the most important aspect of measurement. The crucial factor about measurement is that it is a lever to drive enhanced productivity and performance. It provides the signals you need to determine whether your course is sound or, if not, to course correct. It tells you whether to pull back your investments or to increase them. Measurement helps you hear the voice of the customer — and identify the intentions of future customers.

It also helps you strengthen your marketing operation. You learn how your staff is performing. What outcomes are they generating through their actions? You learn how well your extended team is working — whether that team is in sales, contact center management or retail operations. By gaining insights into campaign response rates or the productivity of particular programs you open a window into the strengths and weaknesses of your marketing operation. You acquire essential feedback to drive your next set of moves.

In order to optimize your programs over time it's not enough to print a lot of reports or produce a thick PowerPoint deck. You and your team must make decisions to take actions based on what the data is telling you. Review and action planning forums can be important rituals to schedule into your calendar.

Martyn Etherington established a monthly operations review for his team at Tektronix. "We mixed all of my regional directors (there were five regions around the world) and all of my operations team. We'd come in and have a four-hour meeting every month to review our financials and our KPI dashboard. And that's when we had robust conversations about continuous improvement. We were really not focusing on the green items but on the red ones where we hadn't met our plan and tried to understand why that was.

"We used a process called the 'Five Whys' to get to the root cause of the problem. Then we'd plan the countermeasures and then they'd become action plans. And then at the next operations review we'd sit down and say, 'Okay, we said what we were going to do and was that effective?' We'd review the action plans but, more important, see if the results were trending back to where they should be."

As you generate quality metrics and demonstrate real progress toward your business goals you'll build credibility and confidence with your executive peers. You'll be able to demonstrate to the CEO, CFO and CRO exactly how marketing has moved the needle since you've assumed your role as its leader. By demonstrating how you've met (or exceeded) your commitments you'll elevate your status — and the status of marketing overall — within the enterprise. And even when you hit unexpected problems you'll be able to explain your challenges — and the ways in which you intend to address them — in the language of numbers.

You'll earn the respect of your peers by confronting reality as it is — not as you (or they) wish it to be. You'll have the facts on your side and the figures at your command. Where there was once excessive uncertainty and complexity you can bring much-needed clarity, perspective and guidance.

ACTION PLAN CHECKLIST

1. Gather the existing measurement reports available in your company.
2. Map out the ideal measurement framework to manage your business.
3. Assign owners to each element in your framework and develop sample dashboards.
4. For each dashboard, determine:

    a) What will be reported daily, weekly, monthly and quarterly
    b) Who will be on the distribution list
    c) In which forums will the data be reviewed and discussed

5. Evaluate the viability of establishing a marketing operations function.

XI.

The latest in technology will not intimidate me but will pique my curiosity and provoke me to find innovative tools to enable sustainable progress.

SYSTEMS FOR
SUCCESS

Jim Davis' route to the CMO position at SAS, a multi-billion-dollar analytics software company, was not typical of many marketers, but was well suited for SAS.

"My education was in computer science, so as a computer science grad I worked for a software developer. I became a director of IT and then a general manager for a business magazine." With that background you might expect that Davis was comfortable using IT systems to advance the impact of marketing on his business. And you'd be correct.

"Most of the systems and analytics we have are associated with either prospecting or servicing the existing installed base. On an annual basis, 70 percent of our revenue is renewal from existing customers. We run a lot of analytics on the customer base looking at their propensity to renew or their likelihood to cancel. We do a lot of data monitoring and analytic modeling on the customer, their particular industry and how long they have been with us. We know the product mixes that they have, the number of tech support calls they have and the number of education classes they have taken. We know if they're a happy customer. We know if they're a customer that maybe we need to reach out to. We know, based on their mix of products, what we ought to cross-sell and up-sell. We have got over 200 products and services here, so we are constantly looking at the mix and adjusting the models and feeding call centers and direct sales channels with that information. So all of the transactional activity around a customer is in the repository, and then our tools can use that to predict behaviors."

But systems that track customers' transactional information are only part of the picture for Davis. Data is also critical to his firm's prospecting activities. "We look at what we can do with structured data and what we can do with unstructured data. The structured data is what you would expect: We have a lot of information on prospects in a repository and we are segmenting our audience based on our data models. Then we are doing a lot of marketing optimization, meaning, how do we approach this particular prospect: Is it through a phone call, is it through three events? Everybody is different so we look at how to optimize for each particular prospect. It is an iterative process for refining the prospect to the point they become a legitimate lead.

"The other piece is social media. We do a lot of unstructured data analysis, a lot of text analytics where we look for patterns. We also look at a lot of sentiment analysis. For example, is a particular segment of our audience around a particular product trending in a positive direction or negative direction in terms of sentiment? It used to be we'd do focus groups once a year in a particular area. Now we look at things on a monthly basis and we look at how it tracks over time."

LEARN TO LOVE YOUR CIO

To engage in sustained and productive marketing initiatives today you need information systems and tools. It is virtually impossible to execute or optimize your marketing plan without them. In fact, research company Gartner Group predicts that by 2017 CMOs will spend more on IT than the CIO. With the increasing importance of technology to marketing many CMOs are finding that their new best friends are their CIO counterparts.

Within your first 100 days it will be important to reach a conclusion on five important questions:

1. Which information systems and tools are critical for your marketing strategy to succeed?
2. Which systems need to be built, enhanced or modified?
3. Of these systems, which ones require your CIO to allocate human and capital resources? And how will you get your needs prioritized along with the numerous other projects on the CIO's must-do list?
4. Which of your prioritized systems can be built, rented or housed by firms that may not require the CIO's resources?
5. Do you have project leaders on your team who are capable of planning and implementing the systems you need? If not, how can you augment your team with either new hires or outside experts?

It's easy to get overwhelmed by the array of tools and technologies now available. And it's not difficult to invest tremendous sums in platforms that fail to deliver an effective return on investment. With this in mind it's valuable to consider the portfolio of system investments that will be necessary to reach the objectives you've set.

To help you think about your information systems priorities I've organized a brief overview of the most common systems you may need to consider. They are grouped by systems that will enable you to engage customers, to engage partners and to manage marketing operations.

CUSTOMER ENGAGEMENT SYSTEMS

The number of potential touch-points for engaging prospective and current customers can be overwhelming. And an increasing number of those touch-points is facilitated digitally and enabled by technology.

For this reason customer engagement systems are often at the core of marketing efforts to drive change and accomplish business objectives. As customers' expectations for "anytime, anywhere" interaction increase and touch-points proliferate, marketing leaders are challenged to invest in systems that enable them to understand, track and interact with prospects and customers with increasing effectiveness across a multitude of touch-points.

Let's discuss some the most critical systems for you to focus on in your first 100 days.

Web Systems. Your website is often your most important asset for engaging your prospects and customers. It's open 24/7/365 and is frequently the first place potential customers go to check you out. It's the one place all of your company's products and services are visible to all your customer segments. It's simultaneously a brand ambassador, a product expert, a customer service representative and maybe even a sales agent that closes the deal. It's accessed via PCs, via tablets and increasingly via smartphones.

This means a great deal of attention needs to go into how your website (or websites) is architected, designed, managed and measured. Is it delivering the experience your visitors expect? Are they able to achieve their intended outcomes? Is it helping you achieve your business objectives? Is it helping you build your brand and accelerate sales? What are the roles of marketing, product groups, IT, customer service and legal in planning and managing the site? These are questions you'll want to answer early on because there are more complex Web-related challenges around the corner.

Among the challenges you'll be facing are:

- Syndicating your Web content to channel partners
- Creating optimized landing pages for campaigns and using methods such as multivariate testing to enhance performance

- Incorporating user-generated ratings, reviews and stories
- Integrating content to and from social media platforms, such as Facebook, Twitter and YouTube
- Deciding what mobile-accessible features should be incorporated in smartphone apps
- Determining what kind of user community you should build and support
- Connecting your customer loyalty program into the site and mobile experiences
- Evaluating what role e-commerce or online ordering might play if it is not currently incorporated
- Assessing how tightly to integrate retail location or channel partner information, such as where to buy and product availability
- Providing real-time lead referrals to your sales team via click-to-call or click-to-chat features or accelerated lead-form scoring and dissemination
- Facilitating repeat contact or retargeting programs
- Enhancing analytics to get better insights into customer behavior

As you can see, there are many facets of Web-based customer engagement. Developing a Web roadmap can help to prioritize which enhancements you can make quickly and which ones will be phased in over time.

Customer Relationship Management (CRM) and Marketing Automation. To support the objective of managing customer and prospect information, companies adopt CRM systems. These systems organize, automate and synchronize business processes, including sales, marketing, customer service and technical support activities. The challenge is to identify and attract new customers while nurturing and building relationships with existing ones.

CRM systems often encompass an array of capabilities. Among them: a customer database, segmentation tools, campaign management, lead management and analytics. When a company has a direct relationship with its customer, these systems are essential. By centralizing customer data a company can track and engage its customers. The data enable the company to treat relationships as assets to be managed and strengthened.

Another factor that's important from a CRM perspective is the ability to manage a relationship across product lines. This helps the company ensure it isn't calling on the same customer with multiple offers within a short period of time. It also helps a company avoid making irrelevant offers. You can leverage your customer data, for instance, to avoid offering customers products they may already possess and offer them ones that track well with their documented (or inferred) needs and preferences.

By segmenting this data you can differentiate your customers. There are many ways to do this. You can segment by demographic factors such as age, income and geography. You can segment by value. How profitable, in other words, is the customer? How great is the customer's potential value? Such factors can be modeled to identify the prospective buyers you most want to reach. You can segment your customers by behavior. If your customer purchases a certain product you can infer what products or services might complement it. Just as Amazon.com can make inferences about tastes and interests you can make inferences about future purchase decisions.

Such models, then, can be plugged into your campaigns via marketing automation systems. Relying on campaign automation and lead-management systems you can optimize your activities and track behavior in relation to your outreach efforts. You can track inquiries, responses rates and sales conversions — observing which campaigns produce which results. Such systems take a great deal of laborious work out of the process, enabling you to mount more frequent, more personalized and more successful campaigns. In some cases you might even score your leads — based on apparent interest — and nurture your buyers through a multi-stage decision cycle.

Whether you are engaging your target customers through direct marketing, contact centers, websites or retail locations, the data you've amassed can help ensure you interact with them in the most relevant and meaningful ways possible.

Direct Communications. Companies are increasingly seeking direct communications with their customers — and vice versa. Customers want to interact with companies in a more personal and individualized fashion.

In recent years such dynamics have not only given rise to sophisticated e-mail and chat communications, they have become an important aspect of social media, such as with Facebook and Twitter, and in mobile-based communications, such as text messaging.

The key is to recognize that customers are seeking more immediate and intimate ways of interacting with the brands they patronize and purchase. By being responsive you can cultivate relationships, deepen loyalty and enhance customer advocacy. These direct communications systems provide vehicles for direct response and instant feedback, regardless of whether you sell through indirect channels or directly to customers.

Of course different people have different communications preferences. By recognizing and respecting these preferences you are likely to have far greater success in your efforts to reach your prospects and strengthen relationships with your customers.

Local Market Activation. For many marketers your objectives may be to get "heads in beds," "butts in seats" or "feet through the door." Driving traffic at the local level is essential for companies with brick-and-mortar locations or branch offices. Often programs to drive these results are the responsibility of field marketing teams or location managers whose responsibilities extend beyond marketing.

Creating easy-to-use systems for these individuals can be challenging. How will they keep location information up to date on the website? Can they tailor offers and invitations that they can send via e-mail? Will they have Facebook pages for their locations? Can they tweet deals to their local followers? Will texting special promotions be facilitated? Having a plan for supporting the local activation of your national programs could provide you significant leverage and improve your overall results.

Customer Loyalty, Advocacy and Feedback. Building on the direct communications capabilities now available you can take active steps to generate customer insights as well as influence loyalty and advocacy.

Some companies are leveraging technologies and services to generate customer satisfaction, customer loyalty and "net promoter" scores. Ideally you will want to know how your customers are responding — and determine which customers are likely to influence others. When customers are dissatisfied, aim to address their concerns or displeasure. When customers seem prepared to act as advocates, encourage and even incent such actions. Customers who write positive reviews on Facebook or express themselves positively on Twitter might be given special rewards or attention, for instance.

Still other companies are investing in social media monitoring solutions that enable them to gauge responses to their brands. Not only can individual responses be tracked but aggregate-level feedback can be collected to provide trends and perspectives.

Voice of Customer Systems. Not only is it important to respond to individual customers, the marketing team must aggregate the feedback, find patterns and suggest changes to improve the business. 3M found that poor customer reviews of a product were due to a faulty part from one of the company's suppliers. By listening to customer feedback the part was fixed and the 3M product became a huge success. Samsung Mobile listened to social conversations about smartphones and the debate between competing platforms. This informed a marketing strategy focused on championing Android users that firmly established Samsung Mobile as a leader in the smartphone category.

There will be many systems available to help you capture the voice of the customer. Some will use internally generated data while others will use data from external sources, such as social media, retail partners and industry researchers. Your task will be to listen to what the data is telling you and package that information for action by your organization.

PARTNER ENGAGEMENT SYSTEMS

Partner engagement revolves around improving communications and enhancing relationships with channel partners, franchise partners, retail partners and other valued intermediaries in the marketplace. The key is to ensure that channels to the customer are well supported and effective.

By providing tools and platforms that enable partners to communicate, collaborate and take action, you have the ability to attract the best partners in your industry and drive increasingly impressive results. Companies that recognize the power and value of their channels tend to out-compete their rivals and provide a superior experience for their customers.

Partner Relationship Management (PRM). PRM systems enhance communications between companies and their channel partners. Web-based PRM systems let you streamline administrative tasks by making shipping schedules and other real-time information available to all partners on the Internet. As with CRM systems, PRM systems enable you to maintain and manage relationships — deepening them and building partner loyalty in the process.

One factor in PRM systems is the ability to manage and distribute leads. Analytics embedded in PRM systems enable you to track how channel partners perform with leads — how quickly they respond and what results they achieve. This can help you distribute leads to the most effective partners and improve the return on your lead-generation investments.

Incentive Management. Marketers frequently use market development fund (MDF) or co-op marketing programs to encourage retailers and other channel partners to complement national marketing initiatives. In this case partners take actions in expectation of being reimbursed or otherwise incentivized. Be aware that frustrations often arise when the reimbursement process is slow and cumbersome.

By smartly managing these incentives you can intensify your partner relationships and create greater market momentum. With authorization, reconciliation and reimbursement capabilities built into the system you'll have what you need to enable and encourage your partners.

Partner Portal. With a secure partner portal you can provide the information and tools necessary to support, train and guide your partners and ensure they perform at their best. Whether they are franchise partners or channel partners they will need training and support resources to act on the new products you've developed and the campaigns you've devised.

Partner portals may incorporate an array of resources and capabilities. Among them: e-commerce, training, marketing tools, promotional materials and sales tools. The portal may be where partners come to order products or get specific pricing on particular offerings. But it may also be where they get the resources they need for promotional and training purposes.

Shopper Marketing. The success or failure of many marketing programs is what happens at "the moment of truth" — the in-store experience. Retailers and shoppers are getting more sophisticated with the use of technology to inform the buying decision. Through the use of digital signage, in-store television networks, tablets for sales associates, mobile couponing or QR codes that trigger videos on smartphones, technology is impacting how your products and services are being assessed.

If you sell products through retailers you'll need to develop a plan for how your systems and those of your retail partners will intersect to improve the buying experience of your mutual customers. You'll need to involve participants from many parts of your organization and their counterparts at your retail partners. The difficulty in implementing such systems is often due more to organizational issues than technology issues, so assigning a project manager with good collaboration skills and determination may be important to make progress in this area.

MARKETING OPERATIONS SYSTEMS

Marketing operations revolve around planning, budgeting, collaboration, pricing and forecasting. Marketing operations systems enable you to tackle the challenges of resourcing your initiatives, measuring performance and exchanging best practices.

Taking on a new role you are most likely trying to figure out how you'll run the marketing function most effectively. Questions about marketing operations – and how to improve them – will naturally arise. The larger the organization the more complex the problem and, in some very large organizations, this problem can prove time consuming.

Operational reporting and internally focused decision making can end up pulling you away from more essential market-focused activities. So it's critical to move fast to get these foundations in place. Only then can you turn your attention to the outward-focused activities that will elevate your brand and generate new growth.

Budgeting. One of the most essential tasks for a marketing leader is resource allocation, authorization and reconciliation. This puts budgeting at the top of your concerns in terms of driving change and strengthening operations.

In some companies marketing budgets might be pegged as a percentage of overall sales, leaving you with a great deal of discretion to decide how they are allocated. In other companies you may have to present a detailed plan and then make the case for various line items.

Fellow executives may want a deep view into how resources will be invested with respect to product lines, channels, geographies and market segments — and how these investments will roll up into an overall budget. This can be a complex challenge. It's extremely difficult to try to keep up with these issues using mere spreadsheets.

But this is only the beginning. Once the budget is reviewed and line items are approved you must open up purchase orders for specific projects. You must begin allocating your budget, launching programs and reconciling expenses with authorized allocations. You'll need the wherewithal to report to the finance group on where you stand in relation to your plan — and the flexibility to make spending adjustments (or reductions) if necessary.

Your marketing operations system should be designed to help you manage these tasks — giving you immediate access to the budget information you need. It should enable you to stay on top of allocations and authorizations, while ensuring expenses have been properly reconciled.

Marketing Analytics. Assessing the impact your various activities have on driving business results is imperative. With the right systems in place your team will have the information it needs to optimize program performance on a regular basis and you'll have the executive data you need to assess the overall performance of your key initiatives.

Performance measures frequently come from various sources, including sales reports, customer databases, Web analytics, campaign tracking, social media monitoring and third-party data. As discussed in the previous chapter, tools to automate your dashboards can be quite valuable. But getting access to the data from various disparate systems is the important factor in building your marketing analytics system. Automation is a bonus.

Marketing Mix Modeling. As you are able to collect more internally and externally generated data related to marketing inputs and performance outputs you can eventually develop more robust marketing mix models.

Large established marketers such as P&G, Coca-Cola and AT&T have made significant strides in optimizing the return on their marketing investments by using modeling systems.

The most advanced tools are able to help with multivariate problems, such as the mix of brand advertising and trade promotions, allocations between broadcast advertising and online advertising, national programs and local activation. While you may not have the data available to populate a mix modeling system today, developing a plan for such a system can be an informative project for you and your team.

Collaboration. When you have a great deal of activity occurring at once your challenge is tracking program effectiveness across markets, product areas and geographies. You want to keep track of what is working and what is not, making sure others in the organization have a chance to share and learn.

You also need a way of managing multidisciplinary, integrated programs. There is frequently a need for multi-department program and project management. How do you are plan and execute complex projects in a collaborative way? Automation may prove helpful here. There are a great many marketing work processes that can be automated, particularly when comments and approvals are important (as in advertising campaigns or press releases).

Through smart collaboration best practices are shared, projects are managed diligently and workflows are streamlined. You can bring together the specialists throughout your organization (and beyond) to ensure work is performed effectively. Rather than having silos of expertise you create an environment in which the sharing of expertise is the norm.

Pricing. Pricing is another element in marketing operations. When marketing is involved in the pricing process you need to model the impact of pricing changes. You then need to get those changes approved and executed. In such cases product and finance teams may need to collaborate to assess the impact on company financials.

There is an array of new technologies that can facilitate such efforts. They enable companies to model, refine, optimize and approve new pricing approaches — adapting to the facts on the ground as they change.

Forecasting. If marketing is involved in forecasting — and it frequently is through the product marketing function — you want the ability to engage in overall demand modeling at both the aggregate level and at the stock-keeping unit (SKU) level. This is particularly important in a manufacturing organization where parts, components or ingredients are ordered in large volumes. The forecast is a complex determinant of overall performance.

Forecasting systems, which are typically integrated with your enterprise resource planning (ERP) system, enable you to predict demand — avoiding stock outs or excessive inventories. Direct marketing and retail marketing organizations often have the most immediate view into such factors. They can track sales volumes, integrating their models into the forecasting process.

BUILDING YOUR SYSTEMS PORTFOLIO

Clearly there are many challenging decisions as to which systems to consider as you roll out your plan and prepare to execute it. You'll need smart systems to automate activities and streamline processes. And you'll need them to scale up your successful endeavors and deliver repeatable results.

By managing your system investments as a portfolio you can determine which aspects of the portfolio deserve the most attention in your first 100 days and which ones are least relevant in this particular timeframe. Concentrate on the systems that promise the highest impact and you'll be in a strong position to execute effectively and reach your stated objectives.

ACTION PLAN CHECKLIST

1. Build an effective dialogue with your CIO.
2. Assess which systems are most critical to executing your strategy:

    a) Web systems
    b) CRM and marketing automation
    c) Local market activation
    d) Direct communications (e-mail, text, social media, etc.)
    e) Voice of the customer
    f) Loyalty program
    g) Partner relationship management
    h) Incentive management
    i) Partner portal
    j) Shopper marketing
    k) Budget management
    l) Measurement systems
    m) Marketing mix modeling
    n) Pricing
    o) Forecasting

3. Develop a roadmap of systems enhancements.
4. Determine staffing and financial resources needed to enhance prioritized systems.

XII.

By remaining resilient, responsible and relentless, we will prove the skeptics wrong and execute brilliantly in spite of the challenges we encounter.

EXECUTING
FOR IMPACT

Technology industry veteran Steve Cullen was no stranger to running an organization when Symantec invited him to return to the company as Senior Vice President of Worldwide Marketing for SMB and .Cloud. Five years earlier he had left the firm to start and successfully run his own small business. So on his return to Symantec he set out to apply lessons learned as an entrepreneur to the challenges of forming a new division for the multi-billion-dollar information security company.

"When I looked at the organization, one of my two top priorities needed to be organizational clock speed, which is: How can we really speed up the way that we execute? So we started by peeling back the layers on every single process to take out what was not necessary to empower people to make decisions, to speed the pace of change and to increase the agility of our organization.

"The second priority was to bring some science to marketing. We were given a fairly large investment by Symantec so the onus was on me to prove that we could invest those funds wisely and get the return that the company expected. One of the ways we did that was by instituting a tool called Marketing Mix Planning. It is an interesting way of looking at macro economics, at how we've gone to market, how we've invested our funds in the past and what other companies in our space have done. We put that into a model and it basically optimized our marketing investment.

"We used data that we had available for the SMB space, competitive data to understand what competitors had been doing and some other macro economic data that related to our model. We did the best we could with the data we had and we got going. We didn't need 100 percent accuracy; we needed 70 to 80 percent accuracy so we could start executing. That was really the object — to just get going. 'Let's learn from it, let's see what it's telling us, let's operationalize it.' If we're building the right organization that's agile enough to adapt to the changes then we should be fine operating that way."

THE THREE "A"S OF EXECUTION

It's no use having a brilliant marketing strategy if you can't execute it. That's a lesson far too many companies have learned over the years. It's less clear whether marketing leaders have always learned the lesson. Indeed, it's not uncommon to be able to articulate a grand vision but lack the commitment and capabilities necessary to follow it through.

Execution can be exceptionally difficult. In the late 1980s when Dell's growth surge began we had several competitors in the market. Companies such as Northgate, CompuAdd and Gateway all pursued direct marketing strategies. It was unclear at that point how this highly competitive market would shake out.

As it turns out, Dell's ability to align its marketing efforts, product value propositions, operating efficiencies and financial model was superior to that of our competitors. Our ability to execute consistently proved to be the margin between success and failure. Execution often proves a bridge too far for companies in today's intensely competitive markets. To realize consistent, profitable growth you'll need to place an overwhelming amount of emphasis on execution.

Based on my experience and interviews with leading marketers I've identified three principles — the three "A"s — that can guide you in your efforts toward top execution. These principles are: alignment, accountability and agility. By acting on these principles you'll be able to deliver on the promises you've made and the expectations you've set.

ALIGNMENT

Alignment is about ensuring everyone who is engaged in marketing and customer-driven activities is moving in the same direction. When it comes to alignment you can begin by asking yourself several questions:

- Is your whole organization aligned around the same objectives?
- Is there consensus for and commitment to the strategy that you have articulated?
- Is everyone prepared to move in the direction laid out in the strategy?
- Are the efforts of your direct and extended teams synchronized or fragmented?
- Are there groups or individuals who are pulling your organization in divergent directions?

When it comes to alignment you must consider multiple constituencies. Among them: producers, staff and partners.

Aligning Your Producers. As you begin to execute your plan you'll be producing product innovations, promotions, advertising, digital content and other marketing assets. You may be relying on an array of producers — many of them external to your organization. Product design firms, pricing consultants, ad agencies, digital agencies and PR firms may all be within your orbit. However, keeping them aligned can be difficult when you are moving fast.

Sequencing is a particular challenge. Marketing leaders are often frustrated by their inability to ensure that relevant materials are produced at the right time to support key business initiatives. Too often materials are produced with messaging that doesn't reflect the latest product iteration. Or the materials are not produced in time to support a new product's rollout because information was not received from the product developers early enough. Given the lead times associated with effective campaigns it's important that the right activity is performed at the right time.

So if a long lead-time project, such as redesigning your website, is an integral part of your new brand rollout, you'll have to make sure your digital agency partners are prepared to take action as the brand campaign evolves. Ideally the brand strategy and messaging are solid before deploying your digital agency to redesign the messaging and imagery on the site. By giving your partners appropriate lead time you help ensure these activities can be sequenced appropriately.

One big problem, especially in larger companies that are trying to move fast, is that everyone associated with the brand engages the marketplace in a unified fashion. Whether the medium of engagement is broadcast advertising, e-mail, a website, Facebook or in a retail setting, the challenge is to make sure communication is consistent. Consistency is particularly difficult to address when your producers are siloed and separate. You'll end up with mixed and fragmented messages that undermine brand value.

To align producers you'll need a framework for multi-department and multi-partner collaboration. You'll need protocols to keep these parties working together actively. Schedule periodic progress meetings to confirm these parties are moving in the same direction and are committed to all aspects of your marketing plan.

By creating a platform or network that enables your producers to collaborate you take a critical step toward effective alignment. Your brand agency, digital agency, PR agency and others should all be in sync. And while these agencies may naturally view each other as competitors for future business, you'll need to make it clear that their success in their current business depends on active collaboration. They should all be committed to a unified direction and consistent messaging on your behalf.

Aligning Your Staff. You face the challenge of aligning your internal staff, departments and organizations with your marketing strategy and plan. The two groups that are often most central to marketing success are sales and customer service. When you are launching programs, products, promotions or price changes it's essential that anyone who interacts with customers be briefed and prepared.

Radio Shack offers a good example of how to align internal constituents effectively. Prior to launching its ad campaign inviting customers to visit "The Shack," company representatives spent time with associates in every store. They briefed and trained the associates so the stores were prepared for the campaign and understood its goals. As a result the company's campaign proved enormously successful. It had rebranded itself and created awareness of its ability to address the needs of today's consumers around electronics issues and products.

Jim Speros took a similar approach at Fidelity. "A huge part of our success was that before we launched anything outside, we spent several weeks educating people inside on what we were going to be communicating and what their roles were for the brand. So it wasn't just about advertising, it was about the very DNA of who we were and how we went to market, and convincing people inside that they were brand ambassadors within the company. We created an internal website just for employees that had all of the new brand assets, all of the communications elements. We got over 17,000 employees to visit the website and spend an average of nine minutes per visit."

Aligning Your Partners. When I speak of partners here, I mean channel, franchise and retail partners. These are the partners who have direct contact and interaction with your customers. They are responsible for building and maintaining these critical relationships.

The challenge here is that companies get so enthusiastic about getting their new programs to market that they forget to set the stage for partner support and customer engagement. Partners require appropriate collateral and merchandising materials. They need training, tools and support. In the absence of such relevant support, they are unlikely to engage in an effective program launch and present your message appropriately.

Whether your target is a retail associate, an independent financial advisor or the manager of a restaurant franchise, it's critical that the right people be aware of what you are trying to accomplish and how you expect to accomplish it. They need to know what actions they are expected to take in order to achieve the desired objective and see that the customer has an exceptional experience.

Imagine you've launched a national advertising campaign that encourages prospective customers to visit their local stores. Should they enter that establishment with certain questions provoked or expectations set by the ad campaign you need to be certain that the retail sales person is fully prepared for that interaction. If that person is unaware or unprepared for the prospects you've reached then your branding and marketing investments could be wasted.

Taco Bell, for instance, did an exceptional job of rolling out its new value menu and then ensuring its training and merchandizing support were effective. With a limited window of time for franchisees to prepare for the changes, the company moved quickly to make certain all elements of training and support were in place. Franchise staff had to be able to produce the items on the menu and relevant in-store materials had to be available.

The orchestration of such components may sound simple, but complexity rises as you factor in thousands of independent franchisees that needed to be supported. The key for Taco Bell was preparing internal staff to execute the program and enable stores to deliver on the expectations set by the campaign.

ACCOUNTABILITY

In addition to alignment comes accountability. To execute well your people, partners and producers all must understand and meet their commitments. Are they getting things done? Are they delivering expected quality? Are they on time? Are they on budget?

Accountability starts with defining accountable parties for the various aspects of your initiative. This requires that you assign responsibilities and clarify key milestones. You must also recognize interdependencies — the relationships that have to be in place so that work gets done.

Of course, it's expected that project lists, tasks and deadlines be assigned to various parties. But enforcing that commitment to these responsibilities throughout the phases of a multi-faceted initiative can be difficult. Several problems can emerge to undermine accountability.

Problems arise when you ask someone to take on a responsibility without providing ample resources to execute it. You'll need to provide the human or financial resources necessary to achieve certain goals. And you'll need to provide enough time to complete the task. To be accountable you must have the time and resources to perform your job well. It can be challenging, however, to allocate resources appropriately in today's demanding, fast-paced and highly constrained environment.

Another problem is executive clarity and action. Decisions must be made at higher levels to make progress on the front lines of business. When executive sign-off is slow it's hard for operational managers and workers to take action. Global companies can be particularly hampered by this challenge. When HQ is in another country and decisions must be handled centrally it's hard to assume accountability in your own country or market segment.

Risk-averse companies — particularly those in highly regulated sectors such as healthcare or financial services — can make it difficult for their people to execute to plan. While it may be in their nature to be wary of risk, such companies' inability to address risk efficiently can reduce corporate effectiveness. Ironically, accountability for risk can undercut accountability for performance.

In addition, hands-on bosses who refuse to delegate tasks completely tend to negatively affect accountability. Micro-managers can destroy personal initiative in others. One marketing executive I spoke with described how her CEO, himself a former marketing leader, was always second guessing her decisions and undermining her authority. It's hard to be accountable when your boss is unwilling to let you make decisions in the first place.

Yet another challenge is managing and enforcing accountability. Unless there is appropriate follow-up, you may not see the results you are seeking in terms of personal accountability. Tom West, former CEO and CMO of JC Whitney offers a good example. As the leader of the direct marketing company he made the decision to shift employee reviews from annually to monthly. This allowed his firm to provide "fast feedback" and ensure that team members were fully on track. With a rolling three-month execution plan each team member was clear what was expected in the next 90 days. As a result of this approach his company experienced two important outcomes. First, employee satisfaction went way up because people were getting timely feedback. They were getting real-time support from their managers to remove obstacles to execution. Second, the business began to move at a far faster pace. Staff members fulfilled their responsibilities far more quickly.

AGILITY

As the pace of change in marketing continues to accelerate, economic and competitive conditions remain uncertain. Despite the uncertainty, companies must move rapidly if they are to survive and win. They must anticipate customers' needs and create innovative responses — and they must be prepared to move on when needs or preferences shift.

One antidote for uncertainty is agility: thinking, drawing conclusions and acting quickly. You made several assumptions in your plan based on the information you had available at that time. However conditions will change and your ability to be nimble and adjust to these changes will be important.

It will be essential to move quickly on the key activities in your plan so that your windows of opportunity do not close. One response to these dynamics is agile product development. Instead of taking years to plan and roll out a product, prototyping begins immediately. The concept applies to website development, social media program development and digital advertising.

Jim Speros of Fidelity put it this way, "Today there is little tolerance for taking long periods of time for developing. You can't let the perfect be the enemy of the good. If you have a strong idea, sometimes having an advantage is far better than having 100 percent of your 'I's dotted and 'T's crossed. If you can get out the door at 80 or 85 percent and get it done four months sooner, I'd rather have that and refine along the way."

Speed of development is just one factor associated with agility. Speed of decision making is another. Obstacles of hierarchy, decentralization, regulation and cultural inertia can make moving quickly and decisively difficult. But if you lead by example, there is hope.

Steve Cullen of Symantec provides an example of the agility he was trying to model. "We had an opportunity to take over the prime advertising spot in the Thursday *Wall Street Journal* by Walt Mossberg's column. The ad space had been owned by one of the communications companies and it was giving up that space. And we had basically 24 hours to make that decision. A number of us were on the road. I was in Europe. My marketing communications VP was at a focus group Chicago. Our agency was in San Francisco. So everybody was all over the place. But we started instant messaging and talking about what the opportunity was, what the reach and frequency would be, how well targeted that insertion would be to the SMB space. We were able to quickly get to some demographic and firmographic data from the agency. And within probably an hour we were able to make a decision just by getting everybody into a collaborative environment online while we were all in different parts of the world. So that's an example of being agile in making a decision and getting going."

Creating a framework for how certain types of decisions will be made can improve agility. Few things inhibit decisiveness more than ambiguity. If members of your team are not clear about which decisions they are empowered to make, which ones you want to make and which ones require broader organizational sign-off, they are less likely to move quickly.

Part of the framework to consider is the continuum of centralization and decentralization. There are clear trade-offs here. While centralized marketing execution can enhance consistency and quality, it can undermine your ability to offer customized and responsive solutions to local market needs. To act with agility you may need to adapt a central strategy to different geographical markets. The buyers may be different. Local customs may be different. You should provide clarity about what elements of your plan remain consistent and what can be adapted. Clarify those times when centralized approval is required prior to execution and what can be shared after execution.

You need to create parameters for team member autonomy and decision making. This enables your team to be extremely responsive to the changing — and sometimes instantaneous demands — of the market. Dell offers an instructive example on this front. When influential blogger Jeff Jarvis published his "Open Letter to Michael Dell" several years ago he was intent on exposing the company's unresponsive behavior and poor customer service. He proved to be a successful provocateur, generating a wave of interest online that went largely unnoticed by the company. After learning its lesson the hard way Dell is now cited as a social media and customer service success story, capable of providing impressive customer care by empowering individuals to respond rapidly to issues that emerge in social media networks such as Twitter and Facebook.

So whether it is defining social media policies, regional communications flexibility, field marketing autonomy or any one of the dozens of functional activities your team manages on a daily basis, the more clarity you provide on the operating "rules of engagement" the more agile the team can be in its execution.

IT'S TIME TO EXECUTE

As you near the conclusion of your first 100 days, you'll realize how quickly your window of opportunity has closed. Your ability to play the "newbie" card is over. Your time to defer decisions has ended. It's time to "put up or shut up." Quite simply, it's time to execute.

Hopefully by now you have taken time to build your alliances, garner customer insights and win support for your strategy. Your organization should be taking shape with the people, processes and systems needed to put your plan into action. From here on, all eyes will be on you to see how well you can execute that plan.

By creating an environment that fosters alignment, accountability and agility your probability for success will increase. Conditions will change. New challenges will arise. Unforeseen obstacles will materialize. But by being a leader who models these three principles, you will inspire confidence that you and your team can overcome adversity and deliver the results your company expects.

ACTION PLAN CHECKLIST

1. Develop a decision framework for members of your team, clarifying which decisions you expect them to make, which ones you expect to make and which ones will require broader approval.
2. Establish a rolling 90-day action plan for each of your direct reports and determine a regular review schedule to assess progress.
3. Implement a cross-functional alignment forum for each of your key initiatives. Provide clear expectations for cross-team communications and collaboration.
4. Recognize and reward team members who model the principles of alignment, agility and accountability.

SUMMARY

And because of the courage of our conviction and the passion for our cause, we will make the future we envision.

SUMMARY

It's time now to go create the future you envision. You've been put in your role to create positive change for your organization and the clock is ticking. Your initial enthusiasm and energy can be contagious, so make the most of it. But you are bound to encounter obstacles along the way; therefore remain resilient and persevere through the difficult days. Your courage and determination can be motivating for those around you.

Let's briefly review the actions in your first 100 days that will set the stage for a successful tenure in your role.

1. You will clarify your mandate, including the magnitude and pace of change you are expected to lead, and will align with your boss and your peers on a definition of success.
2. You will set clear expectations with those on your team about your agenda and how they can best work with you for mutual success.
3. You will listen actively, build strong relationships with your peers and enroll important constituents early in change initiatives.
4. You will distill insights from customers, from competitors and from inside your organization that will inform your strategy.
5. You will articulate a compelling strategy that will align your organization and set it on a path to achieve the company's desired goals.

6. You will structure your team to support your strategy and will make the difficult decisions to realign resources to support the future not the past.
7. You will build a high-performance team by promoting your stars, encouraging your hard workers, reassigning your misfits, eliminating your undesirables and bringing in missing expertise.
8. You will define critical processes that allow your organization to operate effectively across departments in pursuit of your goals.
9. You will develop an action plan that focuses your team on the critical activities needed to implement your strategy.
10. You will establish key metrics to measure your progress and a review process to make mid-course corrections.
11. You will initiate the deployment of information-technology-based tools your organization needs to operate effectively in a digital world.
12. You will model the attributes of alignment, agility and accountability so your team will execute your plan efficiently and effectively.

If you are like most of the marketing leaders I've interviewed, the first 100 days goes by too fast. You are inundated with so many day-to-day issues that it's easy to get distracted and to lose focus on the big picture. My hope is that the framework of this book and the action plan checklists will be both a guide and a reminder for you in your new role.

As your embark on your quest, remember the words of Sir Edmund Hillary, "People do not decide to become extraordinary. They decide to accomplish extraordinary things." I wish you much success on your journey to accomplish extraordinary things.

INDEX

ABOUT THE AUTHOR

John Ellett has a passion for encouraging and supporting marketing leaders who have the courage to be change agents in their organizations. As CEO of nFusion Group, LLC, a digital-centric marketing agency based in Austin, Texas, John has had the privilege of helping some of the country's leading marketers revitalize their brands, transform their digital presence and accelerate their sales, including Anheuser-Busch/InBev, Chili's, Comerica Bank, Samsung and Toshiba. With personal experience as a marketing leader during the early days of the IBM PC and the rapid-growth years of Dell, he provides a unique perspective that has made him a trusted advisor to marketing executives around the country.

John regularly shares his insights on marketing and marketing leadership at Forbes.com and Marketing-Has-Changed.com. and is a frequent presenter at industry conferences and major universities.

John received his formal education at Indiana University's Graduate School of Business, where he later returned briefly to teach, but he attributes most of what he has learned to the smart marketers and business executives he has worked with over the past three decades.

When he is not working John is actively involved with the Austin community and local charities. He is a founding board member and past chair of The First Tee of Greater Austin and the founder and chair of Austin Helps Honduras. He is also a frustrated golfer, an infrequent triathlete, a proud father and a happy husband of over 30 years.

15583641R00115

Made in the USA
Charleston, SC
10 November 2012